TREASURES REVEALED

from the Paul Mellon Library of Americana

TREASURES REVEALED

from the Paul Mellon Library of Americana

Introduction by Robert F. Strohm

Associate Director and Paul Mellon Curator of Rare Books

Virginia Historical Society

HOWELL PRESS

Charlottesville, Virginia

FOR THE VIRGINIA HISTORICAL SOCIETY

Published on the occasion of the exhibition
Treasures Revealed from the Paul Mellon Library of Americana
Virginia Historical Society

Designed by Carolyn Weary Brandt

Library of Congress Cataloging-in-Publication Data
Treasures revealed from the Paul Mellon library of Americana / introduction by Robert
F. Strohm.
    p. cm.
  Catalog of an exhibition held at the Virginia Historical Society, September 20,
2001–January 20, 2002.
  Includes index.
  ISBN 1-57427-122-9 -- ISBN 1-57427-128-8 (pbk.)
  1. Virginia–History–Sources–Exhibitions. 2. Americana--Exhibitions. 3. Mellon,
Paul--Library–Exhibitions. I. Virginia Historical Society.

F223 .T74 2001
975.5'0074—dc21

                                                           2001024545

ISBN 1-57427-122-9 (hardcover)
ISBN 1-57427-128-8 (paperback)

Printed in China

10 09 08 07 06 05 04 03 02 01   10 9 8 7 6 5 4 3 2 1

Published by Howell Press, Inc.
1713-2D Allied Lane
Charlottesville, VA 22903
(804) 977-4006

CONTENTS

FOREWORD

The Virginia Historical Society will mark its 175th anniversary in a few years, a remarkable milestone for any institution. As we begin to plan for that celebration, we are beginning to re-examine our history. And what a history it is, from the founding in 1831, through the travails of the Civil War, to the VHS's emergence as a major research library, museum, and educational institution in the twentieth century.

One key factor already has become evident as we look at our past: certain people stand out for playing a vital role in shaping the VHS into one of the great historical societies in the country. The name of Paul Mellon, therefore, looms large in our heritage. In life, and even in death, he provided generous financial support, helping underwrite major building projects and enriching the endowment. Perhaps his greatest legacy, however, consists of the wonderful *things* he gave to the Historical Society. His strikingly beautiful and poignant "War Horse" statue has become a beloved icon in Richmond since its placement on our front terrace only a few years ago. But his bequest of a large portion of his magnificent personal library is his greatest gift of all. One only has to thumb through the pages of this catalog or stroll through the exhibition "Treasures Revealed from the Paul Mellon Library of Americana" to see just how extraordinary a bequest it was. Great historical societies and museums have great collections. The VHS has long been renowned for the strength of its collections, but the acquisition of so many items from Paul Mellon's library adds a degree of richness to our holdings that elevates them in a way we could only have imagined before today.

What Paul Mellon did for the Virginia Historical Society, as he did for so many other institutions, reminds me of the words of Cervantes: "The gratification of wealth is not found in mere possession or in lavish expenditure, but in its wise application." As if he used that dictum as his motto, Paul Mellon became one of the great philanthropists of the twentieth century. I had the privilege of getting to know him personally in the last decade of his life. Despite his long-standing generosity to the Historical Society, he never set foot in our building until one day in 1993, when he came to see the rare book room we had named in his honor. Until then we had dealt with him only through members of his staff, who were always pleasant but very protective of his interests. He then made other trips to the VHS over the next several years, and without fail, those visits were a treat for us. It did not take long to size him up not only as a true gentleman, but also as a *gentle man*, who despite his great wealth and prominence, made all of us feel at ease.

Since his death I have wondered if one motive behind his trips was, in part, to size *us* up to see if the VHS was a suitable institution to house a portion of his magnificent library. If so, he never let on. But we were deeply touched when we learned that we, along with Yale University and the University of Virginia, had been entrusted as a steward of one of the most splendid collections of Virginiana and Americana ever assembled. If Paul Mellon were alive today, he would be assured that the Historical Society takes its role as steward of his collection as a solemn but welcome obligation. He would also take satisfaction in the fact that his extraordinary manuscripts, rare books, maps, and prints can now be used to advance scholarship and to educate the public through museum exhibitions for generations to come. The exhibition "Treasures Revealed from the Paul Mellon Library of Americana" and this catalog are our first efforts to share a nationally significant collection with the public. We look forward to revealing more treasures in the years to come.

Any project of this scope would have been impossible without contributions from numerous sources. Two great financial supporters of history, the arts, education, and scholarship provided us with very generous grants to underwrite the exhibition and this catalog—the Robins Foundation and The Andrew W. Mellon Foundation. I have often said that I work with a great staff, and once again my high opinion of them has been reinforced. Associate Director and Paul Mellon Curator of Rare Books Robert F. Strohm, Senior Archivist E. Lee Shepard, and Senior Librarian Frances S. Pollard not only played key roles in producing this catalog and exhibition but also ably represented the VHS in meetings with the executors of the estate to determine our portion of the distribution of Paul Mellon's library. As you can see from the contents of this catalog, they did their jobs exceptionally well.

Dr. James C. Kelly, assistant director for museums at the VHS, is an important contributor to this catalog and even more so as the chief curator of the exhibition. Jim and his staff continue their well-deserved reputation for creating and mounting some of the finest history exhibitions in the United States. I also appreciate members of his staff, including Dr. William M. S. Rasmussen, Dr. Lauranett L. Lee, and Bryan C. Green, who contributed entries to the catalog, and exhibit preparators Dale Kostelny and Drew Gladwell. As always, Dr. Nelson D. Lankford, assistant director for publications and education, provided his editorial expertise. On his staff, Dr. Paul Levengood wrote several catalog entries, as did Ann de Witt, who also worked diligently to organize the transparencies of the catalog, which were expertly made by our photographer, Ron Jennings.

Our chief of conservation, Stacy Rusch, carefully oversaw a major conservation project in preparation for the exhibition. Library clerks Jon Bremer and David Ward, and library assistant Michelle McClintick, never lost their good cheer in retrieving books, many of immense size, from the Mellon collection for their colleagues who worked on the catalog and exhibition. And I cannot fail to acknowledge the contribution of my distinguished predecessor John Melville Jennings, who served as director of the Virginia Historical Society from 1953 to 1978. When Paul Mellon was actively collecting rare books, manuscripts, and maps, John served more than once as a valued advisor. I have no doubt that he planted seeds in Mr. Mellon's mind that have borne fruit for the VHS many years later.

Finally, a special word of thanks goes to three people. The first is Beverly Carter, longtime curator of Paul Mellon's collections and coexecutor of the estate, who has been a special friend to all of us at the VHS who have worked with her. William Reese, whose expert services were retained to assist the executors in the distribution of the Mellon library, has become a new and valued friend. Finally, we remember with deepest gratitude Paul Mellon, a great man, a great American, and a great Virginian. Let the words and illustrations that follow serve as our heartfelt tribute to him.

Charles F. Bryan, Jr., Ph.D.
Director and CEO
Virginia Historical Society

INTRODUCTION

By

Robert F. Strohm

In committing his life to, in his own words, "giving away a great fortune wisely," Paul Mellon embarked upon a mission that would prove as exceptional as it was far reaching in its bounty. He was born the child of fortune, the heir to an abundant wealth that even today staggers the imagination. His father, the successful industrialist and financier Andrew W. Mellon, hoped his son would follow in his footsteps. Though the younger Mellon grasped the elements of commerce, and doubtless would have prospered in its pursuit, he had no interest in amassing even greater wealth. Instead, he chose a different path and during his long life gave away more than most could ever hope to acquire. However much the father and son differed in temperament, they both were possessed of a genuine modesty that shunned the glare of public attention. In the elder Mellon's case, this was never more evident than when he gave to the nation not only his fabulous art collection, but also a magnificent building to house it. Even his sometime antagonist Franklin Roosevelt was obliged to note when he accepted the National Gallery of Art on behalf of the country that "the giver [has] matched the richness of his gift with the modesty of his spirit, stipulating that the Gallery shall be known not by his name but by the nation's."

Like his father, Paul Mellon preferred to practice his philanthropy with little fanfare. The sheer magnitude of his largess, however, made anonymity impossible. Over the years he became recognized as a generous benefactor of cultural and educational institutions, a dedicated conservationist, and one of the nation's foremost patrons of the fine arts. He was best known for his support of such institutions as the National Gallery, the Yale Center for British Art, and the Virginia Museum of Fine Arts, but a comprehensive summary of all the worthy causes that benefited from his munificence would fill pages, while a list of all those whose lives he enriched would be impossible to compile. He had, as one art commentator accurately observed on the occasion of Paul Mellon's ninetieth birthday, "done as much as anyone now living to improve the quality of human life."

Along with his many recognized achievements were more subtle ones that escaped general notice but were no less significant. One of the most remarkable of these was his incredible collection of rare books, maps, manuscripts, and drawings relating to the history of the Americas in general and, in particular, of Virginia. A Virginian by choice, Mellon was devoted to his adopted state and once declared to a neighbor that "it is a wonderful place to live, and I hope that whatever contributions I have made have equaled the amount of pleasure I have had from living here." Perhaps this sentiment explains why one of those whom Mellon did inform of his bibliographic efforts was the director of the Virginia Historical Society, John M. Jennings, an accomplished bibliophile. Because of his expertise, Jennings occasionally received requests from the Brick House, Mellon's library on his estate in Upperville, for opinions regarding prospective purchases. By 1966 Mellon was at the zenith of his collecting efforts, and it was then that he confided to Jennings his intent to present, by gift or bequest, a significant portion of his already magnificent library to the VHS. By way of af-

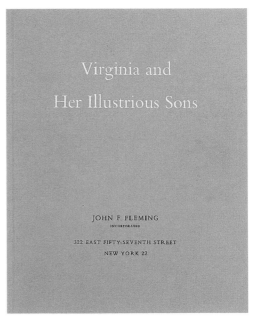

The catalog for the second of two collections of Virginiana, offered by dealer John Fleming, which Paul Mellon bought *en bloc*.

firmation, he gave the institution a list of his library's contents accompanied by a gentle admonition that the Society should make no further inquiry regarding the matter but rather trust to his good intentions and the fullness of time. Within a year or two, other endeavors began to draw his energy and interests elsewhere, and by 1974 he had stopped adding to his collection of Americana. He did not subtract from it significantly, however, and for the next twenty-five years his library became like some exquisite gem, hidden from the world's view. Though he had embarked upon this effort scarcely twenty years before, Paul Mellon had assembled, in the words of distinguished bookman William S. Reese, a "collection of printed and manuscript Americana [that] was the finest in private hands in terms of the quality and quantity of its contents. Indeed, when all is considered, one must conclude that only a few famed collections . . . rival it in quality among collections formed in the 20th century."

Even for a person of Paul Mellon's means and determination, this was a prodigious feat, for only fifty years after he set upon this quest, many of the treasures he had acquired had become virtually unobtainable at any price. How did he do it? To begin with, when he began buying Americana during the 1950s, it was a particularly auspicious moment for collectors with deep pockets and discriminating tastes. The economic plight of Europe after decades of depression and war created a buyer's market, and the energetic private collector with an eye toward value and a modicum of wealth could snare great bargains.

Like most outstanding collectors, Paul Mellon collected thematically and in depth. Unlike the "high spot" enthusiasts who purchase only the instantly recognizable classics, Mellon defined his area of interest and then pursued the printed, manuscript, or occasional artistic works that fell within his guidelines. He did not disdain the fifty-dollar item, nor would he pay what he felt was an unreasonable price for a bibliographic icon. He would not haggle, and the bookseller who lowered his initial offering price to capture Mellon's business seldom sold to him again. Though he constantly added to his collection through individual purchases from a variety of sources, the core of his collection was secured, almost serendipitously, through a few large purchases at what now appear to have been bargain prices. Herein lies a suggestion of the businessman

that he might have become.

Mellon had begun collecting books as a student at Cambridge, and at various times he had built a fine collection of sporting books, pursued works on the occult, and even captured an elephant folio edition of Audubon's incomparable *Birds of America*. His great library of Americana, however, began with his purchase of the J. R. Abbey library, an English collection celebrated for its abundance of aquatint and lithographic colorplates rather than its American content. Yet it did contain a sufficient sprinkling of the latter, particularly American scenes and travels, to inspire Mellon to build on it and to supplement the Old World scenes with those from the Western Hemisphere. One outstanding trophy of Americana that he did acquire with the Abbey collection was George Catlin's inimitable *North American Indian Portfolio*, to which he later added William G. Wall's tour de force of American lithography, *The Hudson River Portfolio*, both of which are featured in this catalog. Other select items gradually were added, but it was not until 1958 that the Mellon collection went, in one grand leap, from being an assortment of choice Americana to one of the most notable private libraries dedicated to that purpose.

It was during that year that New York book dealer John Fleming, with an eye toward the 350th anniversary of the founding of the Jamestown colony, issued a catalog entitled *Virginia's Role in American History*. A former associate of Dr. A. S. W. Rosenbach, the dean of American book dealers during the first half of the twentieth century, Fleming purchased his former employer's stock and subsequently offered many of its most tantalizing items to the University of Virginia. The enormous importance of this collection was not lost upon the university's librarian, John Cooke Wyllie, but he was unable to secure the requisite funding. When a copy of the catalog found its way to Paul Mellon, he purchased its entire contents. One of the most important treasures he acquired is presented here, the 1772 petition from the Virginia House of Burgesses to King George III against the importation of slaves into the American colonies, a hitherto unheralded landmark in African American history. The library underwent another surge of growth when Fleming offered a second catalog, *Virginia and Her Illustrious Sons*, the contents of which

Paul Mellon in front of the Brick House, which housed his library of Americana. Photograph by Heinz Kluetmeier.
Courtesy *Sports Illustrated*.

Mellon again bought in their entirety. Fleming had purchased this second lot with the Mellon library specifically in mind. Among its many prizes were the unique broadside *Glorious News*, which heralded the American victory at Yorktown, and an invaluable collection of manuscripts relating to the Grand Ohio Company and dating from the 1770s. This last was a particularly timely acquisition, because the historic house in which it had been discovered, Uppark in Sussex, England, subsequently burned along with all its contents. With this second purchase from Fleming, the foun-

dation for the library was firmly established.

Though the ultimate disposition of the library was shrouded in silence for thirty-five years, Mellon repeatedly proved himself to be a constant, quiet, and characteristically magnanimous supporter of the VHS. Following up his gift through the Old Dominion Foundation, which substantially underwrote the construction of the 1958 addition to the Society's headquarters, he was again a major contributor to the Fifth Century Campaign, which added the 1992 wing. In 1997 he presented the splendid "War Horse" statue, a poignant memorial to equine suffering during the Civil War that has since become a Richmond landmark. Like so many others who had come to revere his judgment, cherish his friendship, and marvel at his generosity, we at the Society were greatly saddened by the news of Paul Mellon's death in February 1999. In death, as in life, his beneficence exceeded all expectations as he not only revealed his resolve for his fabulous library, but also left the Society a generous financial bequest.

Unlike other collections included in his will that were specifically designated in their disposition, Mellon left the ultimate destination of his Americana, within certain guidelines, to his executors. At the time of his death, this collection comprised nearly eighteen hundred books, maps, atlases, manuscripts, sets of plates, and collections of drawings. Accompanying these were an extensive reference library and other uncataloged, though valuable, material. Mellon directed that his library of rare Americana be distributed among three institutions, the University of Virginia, Yale University, and the Virginia Historical Society, in any manner that the executors deemed appropriate. Throughout his life it had been one of Paul Mellon's great joys and guiding principles to make certain that his collections found permanent homes in appropriate institutions where they could promote scholarship and serve the general public, and this precept was honored in the unusual plan that the executors devised for the collection's distribution. They also were guided by Mellon's oft-stated wish that the Virginia material remain in Virginia, unless it already was held by the university or the Historical Society, and that his library be used to build upon the existing strengths of institutional collections whenever possible.

To accomplish these goals, the executors prepared a catalog of the rare Americana for distribution to the three participating libraries. Each institution was instructed to select those items that were relevant to its collections and not already represented, unless the Mellon copy possessed unique features. Each selection was to be rated on a scale of one to five, with five being the most desirable and with each of the five categories constituting twenty percent of the total number of items requested. Finally, each library was directed to cull from the total num-

The Old Library in the Brick House. Photograph by Steve Tucker. Courtesy Estate of Paul Mellon.

ber a list of its "top ten" selections. Working through the list was an arduous though rewarding endeavor that was highlighted for several of us by a visit to the legendary Brick House. Here, hosted by Beverly Carter, longtime curator of the Mellon collections and coexecutor of the estate, and William Reese, whose expert services were retained to assist the executors, we spent ten memorable hours examining little-known treasures and rarities.

Once the principal residence of the estate, the Brick House had been refurbished as a private museum and library during the early 1960s, some years after Mr. and Mrs. Mellon had vacated it. Their new home, Oak Spring, was constructed within walking distance of the Brick House and lent its name to the distinctive Mellon bookplate. It should be noted that Rachel Lambert Mellon is a distinguished collector in her own right. Her Oak Spring Garden Library is one of the world's great collections of its kind and includes a multitude of celebrated rarities. Until shortly before our visit, the Brick House had been filled with paintings, prints, maps, manuscripts, and books. By the time we arrived, however, most of the rooms were empty except for packing boxes, items being prepared for transit, and the usual paraphernalia that accompany the ordered chaos of moving. Dominating the second floor was the Abbey Room, named for the singular library it once contained. Less prepossessing was a small room downstairs that had once contained the entire library of philosopher John Locke, which Mellon had presented to the Bodleian Library at Oxford University some years before. Next to it was the Old Library, the only room originally designed to hold books and still brimming, floor to ceiling, with the Mellon collection of Americana. Under normal conditions, ten hours might have been sufficient time to survey a roomful of books, but there was also an astounding assortment of maps and nonprint material, much of which had never been published and was virtually unknown. Moreover, some of the printed volumes were unique, or possessed unique features, while others were of such scarcity that the total number of known copies could be counted on one's fingers. As one treasure after another emerged from the shelves and we considered that these were titles almost never seen except in facsimiles and reprints, it was difficult not to linger.

Our labors of love completed and our lists submitted, we were elated to learn several weeks later that the VHS would receive, along with other selected items, nine of its top ten choices and eighty-eight percent of its category-five designations. As a testimony to the wisdom of the executors, both Yale and the University of Virginia were equally pleased with their shares. The good fortune did not end there, for in addition to the 291 items we had selected, the estate subsequently gave the VHS another 248 volumes that, for one reason or another, had not been selected by any of the three institutions. Also received was the comprehensive reference library, as well as books and assorted papers from the library of the noted cartographical scholar Coolie Verner, whose valuable collection the Mellon library had purchased some years before but had not fully integrated. In all, through Paul Mellon's benevolence and the good offices of the estate's executors, the Historical Society acquired nearly two thousand items, including so many unique and important titles that they clearly constituted one of the most important gifts ever received by the Historical Society.

Such extraordinary benevolence merits exceptional recognition, and the Virginia Historical Society is profoundly grateful to the Robins Foundation for sponsoring the *Treasures Revealed* exhibit and the symposium and catalog that accompany it. The symposium, also supported by The Andrew W. Mellon Foundation, is scheduled to be held in conjunction with the exhibit's opening on September 20, 2001, at the Historical Society and will be an extraordinary occasion in itself. Featuring a distinguished assemblage of collectors, curators, booksellers, librarians, and other scholars, it will include speakers who worked closely with Paul Mellon in building his collections and from whose recollections and research I have gratefully borrowed. Special thanks are due to William Reese, whose guidance made possible our productive explorations through the wonders of the Brick House, and for whose good friendship and discerning counsel the Historical Society will always be grateful. His Malkin Lecture at the University of Virginia on July 24, 2000, has been an indispensable resource in the composition of this brief introduction. We are equally indebted to the executors, Beverly Carter and Frederick A. Terry, Jr., for their wise distribution of an estate that was as challenging in its magnitude as it was extraordinary in its contents. Ms. Carter also has been of invaluable assistance in the creation of this catalog by supplying much of the introduction's photography.

Even with such expert guides, it has been no easy task to assemble an exhibit that adequately conveys the depth and richness of the Mellon bequest, or of its importance to the Society's already renowned collections. In our attempt to accomplish this, we have selected approximately one hundred items and organized them into broad themes illustrative of the greatest strengths and most interesting aspects of the collection. This has resulted in a few cases in an apparently disproportionate representation, as with the seventeenth-century imprints concerning the early colony under "Visions of Virginia." As this assemblage of exceedingly rare pamphlets is an important feature, however, it would have been a disservice to the reader to have omitted any more of these titles than we did.

Within the thematic areas that parallel historical eras, the items generally are arranged chronologically. Within others, such as "Virginians at Work," we have allowed ourselves the license to impose such order as seemed logical for the contents. As its title indicates, the exhibit comprises principally, though not exclusively, the bequest's greatest treasures, for we also have included lesser ones to demonstrate the breadth of the collection. Mellon was not averse to the prosaic or the whimsical if it added dimension to his collection, as manifested here by such titles as the venerable *The Children in the Woods* or the charmingly bizarre *Spectropia.* Nor was his library constrained by format, for while the preponderance of the collection was composed of books and manuscripts, as represented here, there was also an indispensable component of maps, prints, sketches, paintings, and even a child's antique puzzle with a fanciful depiction of Pocahontas's marriage.

As several who knew him have observed, Paul Mellon probably would have us remember him as an amateur, in the sense of someone who pursues an interest purely out of love, and as someone whose satisfaction in acquiring was excelled only by his joy in giving away. To those of us at the Virginia Historical Society, the Mellon bequest is both a treasure and a trust, and as Paul Mellon gathered his collections in trust to this nation and the world, so do we look forward to making the contents of this magnificent bequest available for research and sharing its riches with the public. We invite the reader of this catalog to approach it like a visit to the Old Library, lifting each surprising treasure from its brimming shelf, carefully perusing its contents, and then pausing a moment to savor its tangible link to our common past before moving to the next delight. Paul Mellon, we think, would approve.

I. *The Idea of Virginia*

I Thomas Hariot (1560–1621)

A briefe and true report of the new found land of Virginia . . .
Frankfurt am Main: Typis Ioannis Wecheli, svmtibvs vero Theodori DeBry, anno 1590
46 pp. 34 plates

This account of the first attempt to plant an English colony in America is also the first published book illustrated from drawings executed in what is now the United States. It features the work of artist John White, whose sketches represent the earliest authentic pictorial record of life in the New World. It is, in the words of one savant, the "most delectable of Americana." Shown opposite is the celebrated "Adam and Eve plate," considered one of the finest copperplate engravings ever published and emblematic of Europe's hope that the Western Hemisphere would prove a new Eden of peace and plenty.

The author, a mathematician and scientist, had been dispatched by Sir Walter Ralegh as a surveyor with expeditions in 1584 and 1585. The second expedition lasted nearly a year, allowing Hariot and his companions ample opportunity to explore from Ocracoke Island to Hampton Roads. This surviving record of his investigations was written more to promote the Virginia Company than as a scientific report. Virginia is presented not so much as a place to make a home, but rather as a source of riches to be harvested and sent back to Europe. Only after recounting all of the commercial possibilities did he proceed to a description of the lives and manners of the inhabitants.

Hariot's work first appeared as a pamphlet in 1588 but did not reach a wide audience until it was issued in 1590 by Theodore de Bry, accompanied by White's drawings. Published in four language editions, of which the English one is now by far the rarest, the book was a great success and launched the publication of de Bry's exhaustive *Great and Small Voyages.* More importantly, Hariot's account stirred public interest in the New World and probably was a key factor in generating renewed enthusiasm for the Virginia colony.

RFS

Iodocus a Winghe in.   Theodore de Bry f.

2   James I, King of England and Wales (1566–1625)

The Order [banishing rogues to the New Found Lands]
London: Imprinted . . . by Robert Barker, Printer to the Kings most Excellent Maiestie,
1603
1 leaf

    The earliest printed proclamation relating to Virginia, this broadside inaugurated England's policy of
"transporting" criminals to the colonies, a practice that ended only with the onset of the American Revolution.
Crime was a relative term in seventeenth-century England, as there were more than three hundred offenses that
brought capital punishment to the unfortunate offender. Still, there were enough real miscreants among the inno-
cents that transporting felons to Virginia proved an enduring and contentious issue between the colony and the
mother country. As historian Robert Beverley complained of these "Newgaters" in 1722, "As for the Malefac-
tors condemn'd to Transportation, tho' the greedy Planter will always buy them, yet it is to be fear'd they will be
very injurious to the Country, which has already suffer'd many Murthers and Robberies."

    These were precisely the types of "desperate villaines" that James I's Privy Council had in mind when it
issued this proclamation during the first year of the new king's reign, decreeing that "any such incorrigible or
dangerous Rogues shall bee banished and conveyed according to the said statute . . . [to] these Countries and
places following, viz. The New-found Land [Virginia], the East and West Indies, France, Germanie, Spaine, and
the Low-countries, or any of them." Reaction in mainland Europe to becoming the designated dumping ground
for England's criminal class is unrecorded.

RFS

The Order.

Orasmuch as it hath appeared vnto vs aswell by our owne viewes in our trauailes in this present Progresse of his Maiestie, as also by good and credible information from diuers and sundrie partes of the Realme, that Rogues grow againe and increase to bee incorrigible, and dangerous not onely to his Maiesties louing Subiects abroad, but also to his Maiestie and his Honourable Houshold and attendants in and about his Court, which growing partly through the remissenes of some Iustices of the Peace, and other Officers in the Countrey, and partly for that there hath beene no Suite made for assigning some place beyond the Seas, to which such incorrigible or dangerous Rogues might bee banished, according to the Statute in that behalfe made: We therfore of his Maiesties priuie Councel, whose names are hereunto subscribed, finding it of necessitie to reforme great abuses, and to haue the due execution of so good and necessarie a Law, doe according to the power limitted vnto vs by the same Statute, hereby Assigne and thinke it fit and expedient, that the places and partes beyond the Seas to which any such incorrigible or dangerous Rogues shall bee banished and conueyed according to the said Statute, shall bee these Countries and places following, viz. The New-found Land, the East and West Indies, France, Germanie, Spaine, and the Low-countries, or any of them.

T. Buckhurst.	Lenox.	Notingham.
Suffolke.	Deuonshire.	Mar.
Ro. Cecill.	E. Wotton.	Jo. Stanhop.

Imprinted at London by Robert Barker,
Printer to the Kings most Excellent
Maiestie. Anno 1603.

3 John Smith (1580–1631)

A True Relation of such occurrences and accidents of noate as hath hapned in Virginia since the first planting of that Collony, which is now resident in the South part thereof, till the last returne from thence. Written by Captain Smith, Coronell of the said Collony, to a worshipfull friend of his in England
London: Printed for John Tappe, and are to bee solde at the Grey-hound in Paules-Church-yard, by W. W., 1608
42 pp.

This unassuming pamphlet, some claim, signifies the birth of American literature, or at least of American literature in the English tongue. Thomas Hariot's *Brief and True Report* was published earlier but had been written in England. Other accounts of Virginia and New England predated Smith but were never published until the nineteenth century. Smith's own letter to an unidentified associate in England, similarly unintended for publication, was discovered "by chance . . . at the second or third hand" and hurried into print. Clumsily edited and poorly printed, it nonetheless is invaluable as the first accurate account of America's first permanent English colony and, in a real sense, as the first American book.

By the time Smith embarked for Virginia in 1606, his life already had been very full. He had soldiered in the Netherlands and Hungary; he had toured France, Italy, the Mediterranean, Russia, Central Europe, and North Africa; and he had been enslaved in Turkey and Tartary. Fighting under the banner of the Holy Roman Empire, he had defeated three Turkish champions in single combat, for which he was rewarded by a Hungarian prince.

Smith was planning to join the English colony in Guiana when he somehow became associated with the Virginia Company of London and, by May 1607, had landed at Jamestown instead. His initial prospects were not good, for he was briefly made prisoner by the colony's leaders and was finally admitted to the ruling body, only in an inferior role. By September, however, death and incompetence had thinned the ranks of the ruling council, and Smith's abilities raised him to prominence.

Though Smith has been assailed for his exaggerated sense of self-importance, he was not a liar, and an impartial reading of his *True Relation* makes clear that the colony would not have survived without him.

RFS

A TRVE RE-
lation of ſuch occur-
rences and accidents of noate as
hath hapned in Virginia ſince the firſt
planting of that Collony, which is now
reſident in the South part thereof, till
the laſt returne from
thence.

Written by Captaine Smith Coronell *of the ſaid Collony, to a
worſhipfull* friend of his in England.

LONDON
Printed for *Iohn Tappe*, and are to bee ſolde at the Grey=
hound in Paules-Church-yard, by *W.W.*
1608

4 John Smith (1580–1631)

Advertisements for the unexperienced Planters of New England, or any where . . .
London: Printed by John Haviland, and are to be sold by Robert Milbourne, at the
Grey-hound in Pauls Church-yard, 1631
40 pp.

Although not so well known as his *Generall Historie of Virginia, New-England, and the Summer Isles,* John Smith's *Advertisements for the unexperienced Planters of New England* was, perhaps, his best effort from a literary point of view. The years that had elapsed since his Jamestown adventures often had been as frustrating as the years before Jamestown had been rewarding. Not that Smith had been idle, for during this period he had led an expedition to present-day Maine, had embarked upon several more abortive voyages to New England, and had published a number of books and maps. But Smith could not rest content on the sidelines of exploration, and the last decade of his life was vainly devoted to soliciting sponsors for another colony in America. Even the Pilgrims, who in 1620 were pleased to make use of Smith's maps and books, had no desire to take Smith himself with them.

Rejection, for a while, had made Smith a bitter man. Yet by the time he wrote this, his last book, he had become a philosopher, certain that recognition for his essential role in the English settlement of the New World would come eventually, though perhaps not in his own lifetime. Smith's theme, as always, was the desirability of colonization, this time in New England. He included a chronological history as well as chapters full of helpful advice on husbandry, construction, defense, and "incouragements for servants." Also featured is a chapter on religion, a subject given little notice in his other works, and an uncharacteristically reverent dedication to the archbishop of York. Shown here is Smith's map of New England, accompanied by an engraving of Smith executed in 1616. The engraving assumes a special poignancy when one considers that at thirty-six Smith probably was at the height of his powers but at the end of his adventures.

RFS

NEW ENGLAND

THE PORTRAICTUER OF CAPTAYNE IOHN SMITH ADMIRALL OF NEW ENGLAND.

Æta: 37 A° 616

These are the Lines that shew thy Face; but those
That shew thy Grace and Glory, brighter bee:
Thy Faire-Discoueries and Fowle-Overthrowes
Of Salvages, much Civilliz'd by thee,
Best shew thy Spirit; and to it Glory Wyn;
So, thou art Brasse without, but Golde within.

If so; in Brasse,(two soft smiths Acts to beare)
I fix thy Fame, to make Brasse Steele out weare.

Thine, as thou art Virtues,
Iohn: Dauies. Heref:

Simon Passeus sculpsit.

The most remarqueable parts thus named
by the high and mighty Prince CHARLES,
nowe King of great Britaine

HONI SOIT QVI MALY PENSE

Edenborough
Cambridg
The Base
Schooters hill
Sandwich
Dartmouth
Ipswich
Snadoun hill
Bostou
Hull
Point Dauies
Smiths Iles
SouthHampton
Salem
P. Wynthorp
Bristow
Cape ANNA
Fawmouth
Bauerlie
Talbotts Bay
Franncs Ile
The River CHARLES
Cheuyot hills
Claiborns Ils
London
Oxford
Poynt Suttliff
NEW Plimouth
Poynt Gorge
P. Standish
Cape IAMES
Milford hauen
Wels Bay
STUARDS Bay
Barwick

The River forth
St Iohn Towne
Norwich
Leth
P. Kent
Harrington Bay
Cape ELIZABETH
P. Reeney
Pegruis Ile
Heghton Ils
Barty Ils
Gerrards Ils
Willowby Ils

Gunnells Ils
Aborden
Lowmonds
Finets Ils
P Trauers
Pembrocks Bay
Martins Ile

A Scale of Leagues

2 4 6 8 10

Observed and described by Captayn John Smith
1614

London
Printed by James Reeue

44½
44
43½
43
42½
42

5   Theodore de Bry (1528–1598)

[Great and Small Voyages]
Frankfurt: 1590–1634
26 vols. in 10

Among collectors of Americana, few books are more highly esteemed than the great collections of travels and voyages that occurred during the Age of Exploration. Avidly read in their own day by those fortunate few who had access to them, first editions of such grand compilations as Richard Hakluyt's *Voyages* still form the rare and costly nucleus around which serious collections of Americana are assembled. Among these magisterial works, one is generally regarded as the most important ever published, Theodore de Bry's *Great and Small Voyages*, usually known simply as "de Bry."

A Flemish engraver and bookseller, de Bry went to London in 1590 to prepare an illustrated account of French explorations in Florida. Hakluyt convinced him to delay publication of the French expeditions in favor of Thomas Hariot's account of Virginia, accompanied by John White's illustrations of Indian life in America. Hakluyt hoped that Hariot's account would generate public support for a rescue mission to the Roanoke colony.

The book's success did facilitate White's return to America, but by that time no one was left in the "lost colony" to welcome him. De Bry and his heirs enjoyed greater success, for his compilation of illustrated voyages eventually expanded to fifty-seven parts published over a period of forty-four years. Shown opposite is a plate from volume thirteen of the Latin language edition, which depicts the abduction of Pocahontas by Capt. Samuel Argall and his Indian allies. The complete Latin series given to the Virginia Historical Society was once owned by Charles-Pierre Claret de Fleurieu, who directed the operations of the French navy during the American Revolution. Such an edition of de Bry is exceedingly rare, but a set bound in eighteenth-century morocco, as this one is, is almost never encountered.

RFS

VII.
Pocahuntas Virginiæ Regis filia expatiatum profecta, astu
intercipitur, cap. 1. 2. 3.

Ocahuntas regis Powhatani filia, patri apprimè dilecta, ad quendam ex amicis Potaomeckam usque expatiata fuerat. Eodem venit Anglus quidam Capitaneus, Argol dictus. Quem cùm sub ignoto habitu virgo invisere cuperet, is re cum amico suo Japazeo communicata, illam astu in navem suam pellexit. Quamprimum navem conscenderat splendido convivio excepta, lætis confabulationibus exhilaratur, posteáque in cubiculum somnum ibidem captura deducitur. Mane Pocahuntas in navi manere jussa, verborum blanditiis placatur; Japazeus verò donis ornatus cum uxore dimittitur. Postea, cùm Powhatani nuncius de captivitate filiæ allatus esset, ipse verò responsum ultra tempus distulisset, Angli una cum Regis filia, armata manu fluvium ascendentes in Regis ditionem progressi sunt, ut captivos suos vel permutatione facta, vel vi atque armis in libertatem assererent: Toto hoc itinere sæpius à Barbaris petiti variisq; injuriis affecti sunt Angli, præsertim cùm angustias fluminis cujusdam ingressi essent, densum telorum imbrem in illos evomuerunt. Cùm igitur unus ex Anglis in anteriore capitis parte lethaliter esset sauciatus, reliqui, exscensione in terram facta, quadraginta exustis domibus, obviaquæque miserè deprædati sunt, sex insuper Indianis graviter vulneratis aut trucidatis.

6 [Robert Gray]

A Good Speed to Virginia

London: Printed by Felix Kyngston for William Welbie, and are to be sold at his shop at the signe of the Greyhound in Paul Churchyard, 1609
29 pp.

Only the third book published to describe Virginia, this lively piece has been described as a promotional tract for the Virginia Company disguised as a sermon. Along with celebrating the fecundity of the land and the "loving and gentle nature" of the native inhabitants, Gray urges emigration both for the familiar reason of proselytizing and the less commonly encountered one of relieving overpopulation: "But now God hath prospered us with the blessings of the wombe . . . the sword devoureth not abroad, neither is there any feare in our streetes at home; so that we are now [a] multitude. . . . And seeing there is neither preferment nor employment for all within the lists of our Countrey, we might justly be accounted as in former times, both imprudent and improvident, if we will yet sit with our armes foulded on our bosomes, and not rather seeke after such adventers whereby the Glory of God may be advanced, the teritories of our Kingdome inlarged, our people both preferred and employed abroad, our wants supplyed at home . . . and the honour and renown of this Nation spread and propagated to the endes of the World."

One of seven known, this "perfect" copy also bears the bookplate of Thomas W. Streeter (1883–1965), another renowned collector of Americana.

RFS

A
GOOD SPEED
to Virginia.

ESAY 42.4.
*He shall not faile nor be discouraged till he haue
set iudgement in the earth, and the Iles shall
wait for his law.*

LONDON

Printed by FELIX KYNGSTON for *William
Welbie*, and are to be sold at his shop at the signe
of the Greyhound in Pauls Church-
yard. 1609.

7 William Crashaw (1572–1626)

A Sermon Preached in London before the right honorable the Lord Lavvarre, Lord Gouernour and Captaine Generall of Virginea, and others of his Majesties Counsell for that Kingdome, and the rest of the Aduenturers in that Plantation . . .

London: Printed for William Welby, and are to be sold in Pauls Church-yard at the signe of the Swan, 1610

91 pp.

Despite John Smith's able exertions, the first several years of Jamestown's existence were a disaster. The pestiferous location, the unwholesome climate, the fractious leadership, and the mounting hostility of the native Algonquins seemed to conspire to decimate the settlers and doom any hopes of commercial success. To help deal with these problems, in 1609 the Virginia Company obtained from James I a new charter that provided for a military governor with absolute authority over the colony's affairs. Encouraged by this change, "adventurers" financed an even larger expedition of settlers led by Thomas West, baron De La Warr. Crashaw's celebrated sermon eloquently reflected the intermingled anticipations of spiritual and material rewards on the one hand, and sacrifice and martial discipline on the other.

"No great thing [is] accomplished without induring miseries," warned Crashaw. His rejoinder to the concern that only "base and disordered men" would volunteer for service in Virginia must have been as sobering to the prospective settlers as it was intended to be reassuring to the investors: "The basest and worst men trained up in severe discipline, under sharpe lawes, a hard life and much labor, do prove good members of a Commonwealth."

RFS

A SERMON PREACHED IN

Lᴏɴᴅᴏɴ before the right honorable the Lord Lᴀᴠᴠᴀʀʀᴇ, Lord Gouernour and Captaine Generall of Vɪʀɢɪɴᴇᴀ,
and others of his Maiesties Counsell for that
Kingdome, and the rest of the Aduenturers in that Plantation.

ᴀᴛ ᴛʜᴇ ꜱᴀɪᴅ ʟᴏʀᴅ ɢᴇɴᴇʀᴀʟʟ ʜɪꜱ
leaue taking of Eɴɢʟᴀɴᴅ his Natiue Countrey,
and departure for Vɪʀɢɪɴᴇᴀ,
Fᴇʙʀ. 21. 1609.

By W. Cʀᴀꜱʜᴀᴡ Bachelar of Diuinitie,
and Preacher at the Temple.

Wherein both the lawfulnesse of that Action is
maintained, and the necessity thereof is also demonstrated, not so much out of the grounds of Pᴏʟɪᴄɪᴇ,
as of Hᴜᴍᴀɴɪᴛʏ, Eǫᴜɪᴛʏ, and
Cʜʀɪꜱᴛɪᴀɴɪᴛʏ.

Taken from his mouth, and published by direction.

Daniel 12. 3.
They that turne many to righteousnesse, shall shine as the starres for euer and euer.

Lᴏɴᴅᴏɴ,
Printed for *William Welby*, and are to be sold
in Pauls Church-yard at the signe
of the Swan. 1610.

8 Author unknown

A True Declaration of the estate of the Colonie in Virginia, With a construction of such scandalous reports as haue tended to the disgrace of so worthy an enterprise . . .
London: Printed for William Barret, and are to be sold at the blacke Beare in Pauls Church-yard, 1610
68 pp.

Published under the auspices of the Virginia Company at a time when many voices were advocating the abandonment of the colony, this is another earnest plea for its continuance. This tract covers much of the same ground as the Company's similarly entitled *True and Sincere Declaration,* which also was dated 1610 but, having been entered for publication in December 1609, probably was printed during that same year. At the time it was the practice of printers to begin the year in their books at Michaelmas, September 29, so that everything printed between that day and December 31 would bear the imprint date of the following year. Here again the councilors recount the impediments that thus far had thwarted their honest efforts: the bareness of the country, the unwholesomeness of the climate, and the perilous sea passage. These were demonstrated, in the first two instances, by the famine and sickness that had devastated the colony, and, in the third instance, by the shipwreck of Sir George Somers, Sir Thomas Gates, and Capt. Christopher Newport in 1609 upon the Somers or Bermuda Islands. This is the first published account of that shipwreck, which, it has been argued, provided the inspiration for William Shakespeare's *The Tempest.*

RFS

A TRVE DECLA-RATION OF THE
estate of the Colonie in
VIRGINIA,

With a confutation of such scan-dalous reports as haue tended to the dif-grace of so worthy an enterprise.

Published by aduise and direction of the Councell of VIRGINIA.

LONDON,
Printed for *William Barret*, and are to be sold
at the blacke Beare in Pauls Church-yard.
1 6 1 0.

9   **Author unknown**

A True and Sincere declaration of the purpose and ends of the Plantation begun in Virginia . . .
London: Printed for I. Stepney, and are to be sold at the signe of the Crane in Paules
Churchyard, 1610
26 pp.

The first tract to bear the endorsement "Set Forth by the authority of the Governors and councillers established for that plantation," this work is cited by Alexander Brown in his *Genesis of the United States* as containing
more historical information regarding the colony's foundation than any other publication of the Virginia Company, or authorized by it. The pamphlet ascribes the plantation's unsatisfactory state of affairs to storms at sea,
failures in leadership, and natural calamity. "Who can auoid the hand of God, or dispute with him? Is hee fitt to
vunder-take any great action, whose courage is shaken and dissolved with one storme? Who knows, whither he
that disposed of our hearts to so good beginnings, bee now pleased to trye our constancie and perseuerance, and
to dicerne betweene the ends of our desires, whither Pyety or Couvetousnesse carried us swifter."

Concluding on a more positive note, the pamphlet holds out the promise of improved prospects under the
leadership of Sir Thomas Gates and Lord De La Warre and advertises for settlers with specific skills, ranging
from ten fishermen and "iron men for the furnace and hammers" to four "sturgeon dressers" and two "pearle
drillers."

RFS

A
TRVE AND SINCERE

declaration of the purpofe and ends
of the *Plantation* begun in *Virginia,*
of the degrees which it hath receiued; and meanes by
which it hath beene aduanced : and the refolution and
conclufion of his *Maiefties Councel* of that Colony, for the conftant and patient profecution thereof, vntill by the mercies of GOD it fhall
retribute a fruitful harueft to the king-
dome of heauen, and this Com-
mon-Wealth.

Sett forth by the authority of the Go-
uernors and Councellors ef-
tablifhed for that *Plantation.*

A word fpoken in due feafon, is like apples of
Gold, with pictures of filuer. Prouer. 25.11.

Feare is nothing elfe, but a betraying of the fuc-
cors which reafon offereth. Wif. 17.11.

AT LONDON.

Printed for *I. Stepney,* and are to be fold at the figne
of the Crane in *Paules* Churchyard.
1610.

10 Alexander Whitaker (1585–1617?)

Good Newes from Virginia. Sent to the Covnsell and Company of Virginia, resident in England . . .
London: Imprinted by Felix Kyngston for William Welby, and are to be sold at his Shop in Pauls Church-yard at the signe of the Swanne, 1613
44 pp.

The missionary impulse to convert, rather than to exploit or extirpate Virginia's indigenous population, was no better exemplified than in Alexander Whitaker. A noble-minded clergyman from a comfortable parish in the north of England, he has been described as a "man of apostolic zeal for the gospel, and of apostolic sorrow for all men still beyond the reach of the gospel; a man to whom his creed was so vivid and tremendous a fact, that he stood ready to be a missionary for it, and a martyr, even at the world's end." To Whitaker, the exhortations of such fellow divines as William Crashaw came as a cry for help and a personal summons. Accordingly, reported Crashaw in his preface to *Good Newes* in 1611, Whitaker "did voluntarily leave his warm nest, and, to the wonder of his kindred and amazement of them that knew him, undertook this . . . heroical resolution to go to Virginia and help to bear the name of God unto the heathen." By the following year Whitaker had been named minister to the colony at Henricus, approximately twenty miles southeast of present-day Richmond, where he established his residence at Rock Hall. It is possible that Henricus was the site of either the baptism or the marriage of Pocahontas, or perhaps both, and that Whitaker was the presiding clergyman, but the few contemporary accounts are inconclusive.

Though *Good Newes* has been dismissed as yet another public relations attempt to restore confidence in the management of the colony, it also is a source of much useful information and seems sincerely animated by evangelical fervor and patriotism. In 1616 Whitaker accepted a new charge as minister to nearby Bermuda Hundred, but his time there was short, for by 1617 he was reported to have drowned.

RFS

GOOD
NEWES FROM
VIRGINIA.

SENT TO THE COVNSELL
and Company of VIRGINIA, resident
in England.

FROM ALEXANDER WHITAKER, THE
Minister of HENRICO in
Virginia.

WHEREIN ALSO IS A NARRATION
of the present State of that Countrey, and
our Colonies there.

Perused and published by direction
from that Counsell.

And a Preface prefixed of some matters
touching that Plantation, very requisite
to be made knowne.

AT LONDON,
Imprinted by *Felix Kyngston* for WILLIAM
WELBY, and are to be sold at his Shop in
Pauls Church-yard at the signe of the
Swanne 1613.

11   Ralph Hamor (d. 1626)

A True Discourse of the Present Estate of Virginia, and the success of the affaires there till the 18 of June, 1614 . . .

London: Printed by John Beale for William Welby dwelling at the figure of the Swanne in Paul's Church-yard, 1615
69 pp.

Hamor's narrative, one of the most informative from the colony's early days, covers the period of his first residency in Virginia, roughly from 1612 to mid-year 1614, when he returned to England. A clear and dispassionate account of Lt. Gov. Sir Thomas Dale's efforts to reform and bring order to the colony, it is also the first and chief source for information on John Rolfe's introduction of marketable tobacco to Virginia and of his marriage to Pocahontas, the newly baptized Lady Rebecca. Appended to Hamor's account are three printed letters: one signed Thomas Dale; the second from Alexander Whitaker, the clergyman who may have officiated at the wedding of Rolfe and Pocahontas; and the last from Rolfe to Dale, explaining that he wished to marry Pocahontas not from "unbridled desire of carnall affection; but for the good of this plantation, for the honour of our countrie, for the glory of God, for my owne salvation, and for the converting to the true knowledge of God and Jesus Christ, an unbeleeving creature, namely Pokahuntas."

In 1617 Hamor returned from England to the colony, where he died in 1626.

RFS

A TRVE
DISCOVRSE OF THE
PRESENT ESTATE OF VIRGINIA, and the successe of the affaires there till the 18 of *Iune*. 1614.

TOGETHER.

WITH A RELATION OF THE seuerall English townes and forts, the assured hopes of that countrie and the peace concluded with the *Indians*.

The Christening of *Powhatans* daughter and her mariage with an English-man.

Written by RAPHE HAMOR the yonger, late Secretarie in that Colony.

Alget, qui non ardet.

Printed at London by IOHN BEALE for WILLIAM WELBY dwelling at the signe of the *Swanne* in *Pauls* Church-yard. 1615.

12   Edward Waterhouse

A Declaration of the State of the Colony and Affaires in Virginia. With a Relation of the Barbarous Massacre in the time of peace and League, treacherously executed by the Natiue Infidels upon the English, the 22 of March last . . .

London: Imprinted . . . by G. Eld, for Robert Mybourne, and are to be sold at his shop, at the great South doore of Pauls, 1622

54 pp.

Though the colonists' mortality rate still was staggering at the beginning of 1622, life in Virginia was gradually improving and the number of its English inhabitants increasing. And even though James I and many of his countrymen considered tobacco to be noxious, foul, and immoral, in just six years the "sottweed" had transformed the colony's economic prospects. Other industries were taking root as well, as the governor and treasurer in Virginia sent "assurance of ouer-comming and bringing to perfection in this yeare, the Iron-works, Glasse-works, Salt-works [along with] the plentifull sowing of all sorts of English graine with the Plough." Most important, a lasting peace seemed to have been forged between the English and the Algonquins. "Such was the conceit of firme peace and amitie," continued Waterhouse, "that there was seldome or neuer a sword worne, and a Peece [firearm] seldomer, except for a Deere or Fowle."

This period of apparent harmony ended abruptly on March 22, 1622, when the Indians, alarmed at the growing number of settlers and the consequent encroachment on their way of life, launched a coordinated surprise attack on the English settlements that left 340 dead, one-sixth of the entire white population of Virginia. A warning by a friendly Indian named Chanco saved Jamestown, but the uprising of 1622 did not just destroy the thriving satellite plantations, it convinced many in England to abandon a policy of relative accommodation for one of bloody confrontation. In an altogether too gleeful inversion of the swords to plowshares proverb, Waterhouse reflected that "We, who hitherto haue had possession of no more ground then their waste, and our purchase at a valuable consideration to their owne contentment, gained; may now by right of Warre, and law of Nations, inuade the Country, and destroy them who sought to destroy vs."

Waterhouse's *Declaration* was the first authorized and detailed account of this pivotal event in Virginia's history.

RFS

A DECLARATION

OF
THE STATE OF THE
Colony and Affaires in *VIRGINIA*.

WITH
A RELATION OF THE BARBA-
rous Maſſacre in the time of peace and League,
treacherouſly executed by the Natiue Inſidels
vpon the Engliſh, the 22 of *March* laſt.

Together with the names of thoſe that were then maſſacred;
that their lawfull heyres, by this notice giuen, may take order
for the inheriting of their lands and eſtates in
VIRGINIA.

AND
A TREATISE ANNEXED,
Written by that learned *Mathematician* Mr. *Henry
Briggs*, of the Northweſt paſſage to the South Sea
through the Continent of *Virginia*, and
by *Fretum Hudſon*.

Alſo a Commemoration of ſuch worthy Benefactors as haue contributed their Chriſtian Charitie towards the aduancement of the Colony.

*And a Note of the charges of neceſſary prouiſions fit for euery man that
intends to goe to* VIRGINIA.

Publiſhed by Authoritie.

Imprinted at *London* by *G. Eld*, for *Robert Mylbourne*, and are to be
ſold at his ſhop, at the great South doore of *Pauls*. 1622.

13 Charles I, King of England and Wales (1600–1649)

By the King. A Proclamation against the disorderly Transporting His Maiesties Subjects to the Plantations within the parts of America

London: Imprinted . . . by Robert Barker, Printer to the Kings most Excellent Maiestie: And by the Assignes of John Bill, 1637

1 leaf

In this curious document Charles I, who succeeded his father, James I, to the throne in 1625, sought to restrain from leaving England those "idle and refractory humors, whose onely or principall end is to live as much as they can without the reach of authority." To achieve this, the king directed that "all the Officers and Ministers of his severall ports . . . doe not hereafter permit or suffer any persons, being Subsidie men, or of the value of Subsidie men, to embarque themselves in any of the said Ports, or the members thereof, for any of the said Plantations, without License from his Maiesties' Commissioners for Plantations."

A "subsidie man," in seventeenth-century parlance, was someone who could afford to pay subsidies, which were taxes that the king could levy directly on his subjects to meet special needs without the usual intercession of Parliament. He was, in short, a taxpayer. By the time this edict was issued in 1637, Charles had been governing and taxing England without Parliamentary assistance for nine years, having dissolved the contentious legislature over an array of religious, political, and military policy disagreements. Taxes were never popular, but the one at issue in 1637, levied to raise "ship money," was especially hated. In the first place, it was excessive: as much as fourteen to fifteen times the amount of former subsidies, according to one account. Moreover, as if to add insult to injury, the feckless navies underwritten by these subsidies sailed from one disaster to another in two losing war efforts.

Despite the king's assurance that he did not mean to burden the poor with this tax, it often bore most heavily upon them, and rather than pay or have their goods confiscated, they fled to the American plantations. In swelling the wave of migration, this last effort of Charles I to wring money from his subjects was as beneficial to the colonies as it was detrimental to himself. Only two years later the king faced an armed rebellion that led ultimately to his execution.

RFS

¶ By the King.

¶ A Proclamation againſt the diſorderly Tranſport-
ing His Maieſties Subiects to the Plantations within
the parts of *America*.

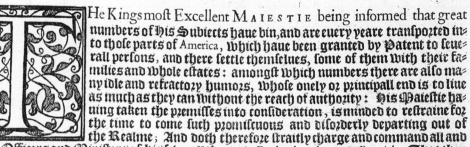

He Kings moſt Excellent MAIESTIE being informed that great numbers of His Subiects haue bin, and are euery yeare tranſported in-to thoſe parts of America, which haue been granted by Patent to ſeue-rall perſons, and there ſettle themſelues, ſome of them with their fa-milies and whole eſtates: amongſt which numbers there are alſo ma-ny idle and refractory humors, whoſe onely or principall end is to liue as much as they can without the reach of authority: His Maieſtie ha-uing taken the premiſſes into conſideration, is minded to reſtraine for the time to come ſuch promiſcuous and diſorderly departing out of the Realme; And doth therefore ſtraitly charge and command all and euery the Officers and Miniſters of his ſeuerall Ports in England, Wales, and Barwick, That they doe not hereafter permit or ſuffer any perſons, being Subſidie men, or of the value of Subſidie men, to embarque themſelues in any of the ſaid Ports, or the members thereof, for any of the ſaid Plantations, without Licence from His Maieſties Commiſſioners for Plantations firſt had and obtained in that behalfe; Nor that they admit to be embarqued any perſons under the degree or value of Subſidy-men, without an Atteſtation or Certificate from two Juſtices of the Peace liuing next the place where the party laſt of all, or lately then before dwelt, that he hath taken the Oaths of Supremacie, and Allegiance, and like Teſtimony from the Miniſter of the Pariſh of his conuerſation and conformity to the Orders and diſcipline of the Church of England. And fur-ther His Maieſties expreſſe will and pleaſure is, That the Officers and Miniſters of his ſaid ſe-uerall Ports, and the Members therof, do returne to His Maieſties ſaid Commiſſioners for Plan-tations euery halfe yeare a particular and perfect Liſt of the names and qualities of all ſuch per-ſons as ſhall from time to time be embarqued in any of the ſaid Ports for any of the ſaid Plantati-ons. And of theſe His Maieſties Royall Commands, all the Officers and Miniſters of His ſaid Ports, and the Members thereof are to take care, as they will anſwer the neglect thereof at their perils.

Giuen at Our Court at Whitehall the laſt day of Aprill, in the thirteenth yeare of Our Reigne.

God ſaue the King.

¶ Imprinted at London by Robert Barker, Printer
to the Kings moſt Excellent Maieſtie: And by the
Aſſignes of IOHN BILL. 1637.

14   William Bullock (b. 1617?)

Virginia Impartially examined, and left to publick view, to be considered by all judicious and honest men . . .
London: Printed by John Hammond, and to be sold at his house over-against S. Andrews
Church in Holborne, 1649
66 pp.

This tract is typical of the many that were intended either to advertise the colony or to turn a profit by endeavoring to supply information then in demand. It differs from the century's earlier promotional literature primarily in tone. Though the colony's previous troubles were too well known in England to be denied or ignored, as earlier pamphleteers had tried to do, its prospects finally were beginning to show real promise. Virginia's population was at last beginning to grow, and its institutions were taking form. Blaming the colony's past problems on the "failings of the first adventurers," and specifically censuring its dependence upon tobacco, Bullock reveals an antagonism toward Virginia's leadership that seems to have derived in equal measure from ship captains' reports and a personal grudge. "When you have read this over," he disclaims in a prefatory letter addressed to the colony's governor and council, "you'll find my love hath swallowed up my loss."

William Bullock probably was the son of Hugh Bullock of London, who owned land in York County and resided there for a time. The author inherited this property, including a sawmill and a plantation, but seems never to have occupied it.

RFS

VIRGINIA

Impartially examined, and left to publick view, to be considered by all Iudicious and honest men.

Under which Title, is comprehended the Degrees from 34 to 39, wherein lyes the rich and healthfull Countries of *Roanock,* the now Plantations of *Virginia* and *Mary-land.*

Looke not upon this BOOKE, as those that are set out by private men, for private ends; for being read, you'l find, the publick good is the Authors onely aime.

For this Piece is no other then the Adventurers or Planters faithfull Steward, disposing the Adventure for the best advantage, advising people of all degrees, from the highest Master, to the meanest Servant, how suddenly to raise their fortunes.

Peruse the Table, and you shall finde the way plainely lay'd downe.

By WILLIAM BULLOCK, Gent.

19 *April,* 1649. *Imprimatur,* Hen: Whaley.

LONDON:

Printed by *John Hammond,* and are to be sold at his house over-against S. *Andrews* Church in *Holborne.* 1649.

15 Author unknown

The Lord Baltemores Case, Concerning the Province of Maryland, adjoyning to Virginia in America . . .
London: n.p., 1653
20 pp.

One of only five copies known to exist, this tract recounts the trials of Cecil Calvert, the second baron Baltimore, in defending his Maryland proprietary against claims from Virginia. The entire territory of Maryland, the charter for which was granted to Calvert in 1632, had been included in earlier grants made to the Virginia Company. Though the Virginians had established no permanent settlements north of the Potomac River, they objected to the partitioning of land they considered their own. The chief agitator was one William Clayborne, or Claiborne, who had established a trading post on Kent Island in the Chesapeake Bay. When commanded to submit to the new government, he and his followers resorted to arms, were defeated, and fled to Virginia to await future opportunities for retribution.

That opportunity came with the Puritan Revolution, when the governor of Maryland, following Sir William Berkeley's example in Virginia, proclaimed continuing allegiance to the crown. Like Berkeley, he was deprived of his office in favor of a group of commissioners, which included Calvert's nemesis, William Clayborne. Clayborne and his cohorts attempted to reassert Virginia's claim to some of Calvert's proprietary but were rebuffed, in large measure because of this eloquently reasoned argument that it would be more advantageous to England to retain Maryland as a separately governed entity.

RFS

THE LORD

BALTEMORE'S

CASE,

Concerning the Province of *Maryland*, adjoyning to *Virginia* in *AMERICA*.

With full and clear Anſwers to all material Objections, touching his Rights, Juriſdiction, and Proceedings there.

And certaine Reaſons of State, why the Parliament ſhould not impeach the ſame.

Unto which is alſo annexed, a true Copy of a Commiſſion from the late King's Eldeſt Son, to Mr. *William Davenant*, to diſpoſſeſſ the Lord *Baltemore* of the ſaid Province, becauſe of his adherence to this Common-Wealth.

LONDON,

Printed in the Yeare, 1653.

16   Lionel Gatford (d. 1665)

Publick Good Without Private Interest or, A Compendious Remonstrance of the present State and Condition of the English Colonie in Virginea . . .

London: Printed for H. Marsh, and are to be sold at the Crown in S. Paul's Church-yard, 1657

26 pp.

In this remarkably rare pamphlet, one of only four copies known, Gatford produced an argument that is notable not so much for its premise or proposed remedies, as for the vehemence with which it is delivered. Virginia had brought "shame and dishonour" upon England largely, he opined, because of its popular government and the "inseparable unhappiness and mischief that constantly attends both the Gouvernours and Governed, where the power of the Gouvernour depends upon the favour and pleasure of the people." For too many years, Gatford argued, the self-seeking colonists had been free to gratify their own appetites and ambitions, drinking excessively, living where and how they pleased, cultivating tobacco to their hearts' content, warring with the Indians when it suited them, and generally ignoring London's efforts to make them mend their ways. What was needed was a reorganization that would give the authorities in England nearly absolute power to coerce the wayward colonists into pursuing "publick good" rather than "private interest."

A merchant familiar with the Chesapeake trade and its affairs, Gatford never actually visited Virginia.

RFS

PUBLICK
GOOD
Without Private
INTEREST:

OR,

A Compendious *Remonstrance* of the
preſent ſad State and Condition of the Engliſh
Colonie in VIRGINEA.

WITH

A Modeſt DECLARATION of the ſeverall Cauſes
(ſo far as by the Rules of Right, Reaſon, and Religious Obſer-
vation may be Collected) why it hath not proſpered better hitherto

AS ALSO,

A Submiſſive ſuggeſtion of the moſt prudentiall probable wayes, and
meanes, both Divine and Civill (that the inexpert Remembrancer could
for the preſent recall to minde) for its happyer improvement
and advancement for the future.

Humbly preſented to His Highneſs the Lord *Protectour*,
By a Perſon zealouſly devoted,
To the more effectual propagaing of the Goſpel in that Nation,
and to the inlargement of the Honour and Benefit, both of the ſaid
Colonie, and this whole Nation, from whence they
have been tranſplanted.

Qui ſibi ſoliim ſe natum putat,
ſecum ſolus ſemper vivat,
Hoc ſolum habent homines cum deo commune,
Alius bene facere Synes.
To do good, and to communicate, forget not:
for with ſuch ſacrifices, God is well pleaſed, *Heb.* 13. v. 16.

LONDON,
Printed for *Henry Marſh*, and are to be ſold at
the Crown in S. *Paul's* Church-yard. 1657.

17　Francis Moryson (fl. 1628–1680)

The Lawes of Virginia Now in Force. Collected out of Assembly Records, and Digested into one Volume. Revised and Confirmed by the Grand Assembly held at James City, by Prorogation, the 23d of March 1661. In the 13th Year of the Reign of our Soveraign Lord King Charles the II

London: Printed by E. Cotes, for A. Seile over against St. Dunstans Church in Fleet-street, 1662

82 pp.

Deputy governor of the Virginia colony from 1661 to 1662, Moryson apparently served as an officer in the Royalist army during England's civil war and, when the king's cause was lost, emigrated to Virginia in 1649. As a fellow Royalist, Moryson found favor with Virginia's governor, Sir William Berkeley, and soon became a figure of local importance. Beginning as commander of the fort at Old Point Comfort, as well as a member of the Virginia Council, he later served as speaker of the house on several occasions and, by 1661, had been put in charge of Virginia's affairs as acting governor while Berkeley traveled to England to plead the colony's economic case against the increasingly restrictive Navigation Acts.

His most lasting accomplishment as acting governor was this compilation and revision of Virginia's laws, undertaken at Berkeley's direction, which was finished on schedule despite numerous distractions. The work "might, perhaps, have been better done," reported Moryson, "had not the Troubles of the Indians, and Quakers, and other emergent Occasions of the Publique, depriv'd me of much of that time I had devoted to that most serious Imployment."

Moryson made several more transatlantic crossings on behalf of crown and colony, once as a commissioner to investigate the causes of Bacon's Rebellion, and later retired to England.

RFS

THE
LAWES
OF
VIRGINIA
Now in Force:

Collected out of the *Assembly Records*, and
Digested into one Volume.

Revised and Confirmed by the *Grand Assembly*
held at *James=City*, by Prorogation, the 23d of
March 1661. in the 13th. Year of the Reign
of our Soveraign Lord

King Charles the II.

LONDON:

Printed by *E. Cotes*, for *A. Seile* over against
St. *Dunstans* Church in *Fleet-street*. M. DC. LXII.

18   John Ogilby (1600–1676)

America: Being the Latest, and Most Accurate Description of the New World; Containing the Original of the Inhabitants, and the Remarkable Voyages thither . . .
London: Printed by the Author, and are to be had at his House in White Fryers, 1671
674 pp.

Present here in the exceedingly rare first issue of the first edition, Ogilby's *America* was the first encyclopedia of the New World to be published in the English language and earned its author the sobriquet of "the English de Bry." It was but one part of an even more ambitious multivolume work that was intended by its author to encompass the entire known world, with a volume each devoted to America, Africa, Asia, and Europe, along with six more devoted entirely to Great Britain. Such a monumental endeavor would have been remarkable for any individual under the most favorable conditions, but it is even more amazing when one considers that the author was sixty-nine years old and, only a few years earlier, had lost everything in the great London fire.

Of the intended foreign atlases, Ogilby managed to complete Africa, America, and part I of Asia. The American atlas is considered to be his best, even though so much of it was appropriated from a contemporary, Arnoldus Montanus, that one bibliographer was moved to call it "an impudent plagiarism." For example, the highly embellished title page shown here is identical to the one used by Montanus. Yet, if Ogilby was guilty of overzealous borrowing, a common practice among the freebooting literary opportunists of his day, he also made many textual additions and changes, as well as adding several new maps. However mixed its pedigree, Ogilby's lavishly illustrated account of the American continents proved a great commercial success with a public hungry for the accounts of those "Expert and Stout Captains" who had "Furrow'd . . . [that] Watry part of the World, that almost through all the Ages" had lain "Fallow."

RFS

AMERICA

19 William Byrd (1652–1704)

Letter, June 21, 1688, to William Blathwayt at the Plantation Office at White Hall,
London, England
Manuscript
1 p.   11 x 7 in.

William Byrd I came to Virginia sometime before 1670 to live with his childless uncle, Thomas Stegge, auditor general of the colony. Quickly adapting to Virginia's frontier as an explorer, fur trader, and militia officer, Byrd secured election to the House of Burgesses at a relatively young age and soon thereafter appointment to the Governor's Council. Still ambitious, he traveled to England in 1687 seeking to follow in his uncle's footsteps by purchasing the lucrative office of Virginia's deputy auditor and receiver general of revenues.

The post Byrd sought had long been held by Nathaniel Bacon, Sr. (1620–1692), a cousin of his rebellious namesake. Bacon had announced his intention to relinquish the auditor's office a year earlier, citing age and declining health. The timing and nature of this transfer of authority, however, along with questions about the equitable division of fees, briefly tarnished relations between the two men. As Byrd notes in this letter to the "Receiver General of His Majesty's Revenue in Foreign Plantations," William Blathwayt: "Hee Saith as his voluntary Surrender was necessary, so hee is not to Acco[un]t for any thing to mee, relating to any part of his Ma[jes]tys revenue now in his hands; this I presumed to acquaint you with, that you might bee sensible how affairs stand between us."

Some sense of the importance of colonial offices to the rising gentry class may be gained from the fact that in 1688 Byrd also purchased the twelve hundred acres that would later be known as Westover Plantation.

ELS

Honoble Sr

I made bold to trouble you about
a month Since, wherein I gaue you an Accot that
Colt Bacon did promiss to Surrender the Audito:
place this moneth; wch hee Accordingly did
yesterday, & I was Sworne & gaue Security for
Officiating the Same; Hee Saith as his voluntary
Surrender was necessary, So hee is not to Accot
for any thing to mee, relating to any part of his Matjes
revenue now in his hands; this I presumed to
acquaint you with, that you might bee sensible
how affairs Stand between us.

I must again beg your favorable Assistance if
Mr Ayleway should make any Stay about his Patent

I humbly beg pardon for this trouble, & take leaue
Assureing you I am on all Occasions

Honod Sr
Yor most Obledged
Humble Servant

Wm Byrd

To the Honod Wm
Blathwait Esqr: att
the Plantation Office
at White hall
These humbly present

Virg 21 June 1698
From Coll Byrd
Recd 10 Augst 98

II. *A Clash of Empires*

20　Louis Hennepin (1640–1705?)

A New Discovery of A Vast Country in America, Extending about Four Thousand Miles, Between New France and New Mexico . . .
London: Printed for M. Bentley, J. Tonson, H. Bonwick, T. Goodwin, and S. Manship, 1698
228 pp.

Louis Hennepin, a young Franciscan missionary-priest, sailed to Quebec in 1675 aboard the same vessel that carried René Robert Cavelier de La Salle. Hennepin served as an itinerant missionary in various colonial settlements in New France. In the fall of 1678, he accompanied La Salle into the Great Lakes region. During their journey, Hennepin was captured by Sioux Indians and traveled extensively with them until his rescue in 1681.

Hennepin returned to France in 1682, where he published *Description Louisiane* (1683), a detailed account of his North American adventures that earned him considerable acclaim in Europe. In 1687 and 1692, Hennepin was forced to flee positions in France under mysterious circumstances, which caused him to seek the protection of King William III of England. With British assistance, Hennepin published in Utrecht two major works on early North America, *Nouvelle découverte...* (1697) and *Nouveau Voyage...* (1697). This English translation from the Mellon library was published the following year. In these works, Hennepin falsely claimed to have made a voyage of discovery along the lower Mississippi River before La Salle's famous descent in 1682.

Hennepin's three books were translated into numerous languages in more than forty editions. The first book helped focus attention on the importance of Mississippi Valley exploration and development. The latter two books, based substantially on fallacious information, largely destroyed Hennepin's reputation as a writer and authority on North American exploration. However, the works had a profound effect on North American colonization.

As the natural range of the American bison extended as far south as Florida, the visually unlikely conjunction of pelican and bison illustrated here was actually plausible. Hennepin marveled at the scene created by extensive herds of bison. Their "Ways," he recalled, were "as beaten as our great Roads, and no Herb grows therein" (p. 92).

BCG

21 George Washington (1732–1799)

Letter, March 20, 1754, to Lt. Gov. Robert Dinwiddie of Virginia
Manuscript
3 pp. 7 x 9 in.

Instructed by Governor Dinwiddie in the fall of 1753 to evaluate the French military presence along the Ohio River and deliver a letter requesting their departure from the region, twenty-two-year-old George Washington returned from his mission to both official and popular acclaim. Accepting a commission as lieutenant colonel of Virginia forces, he wrote in typically self-effacing eighteenth-century fashion of his intention "strictly to adhere to all the proper Rules (as far as it is in my power) and discipline of the Profession I have now enter'd into; I am vain enough to believe, I shall not be quite an unfit Member for it; but in time, shall be able to recompense for the present indulgences."

Washington was busy gathering recruits for the Virginia Regiment in anticipation of an expedition against the French. The offer of bounty lands had brought together "a number of selfwill'd, ungovernable People" that Washington labored to form into a cohesive unit. Within a few weeks he would set out on a mission that would lead to a series of confrontations with the French; the controversial killing of one of their commanders, the sieur de Jumonville; and Washington's own surrender of Fort Necessity. Ultimately, some observers in England laid responsibility for the start of the Seven Years' (or French and Indian) War squarely at Washington's feet.

The Virginia Historical Society acquired an extensive series of the correspondence from this period between Washington and Dinwiddie in 1881 through the gift of William W. Corcoran. This important letter fills a significant gap in that set of papers.

ELS

Honble Sir

      I was favour'd with your Honours Letter by Mr Steward, inclosing a Lieu^t Col^o.—Commission, for which Promotion, I hope, my future Behaviour will sufficiently testifie the true sense I have of the Kindness, and as I intend strictly to adhere to all the proper Rules (as far as it is in my power) and discipline of the Profession I have now enter'd into; I am vain enough to believe, I shall not be quite an unfit Member for it, but in time, shall be able to recompense for the present indulgences — At this time there is ab^t 75 Men at Alexandria near 50 of which I have Enlisted, the others have been sent by Messrs Polson, Mercer and Waggoner to this place; there is very few Officers repair'd hither yet, which has occasion'd a very fatieguing time to me, to manage a number of selfwill'd, ungovernable People, I shall implicitly

March 20 1754
G. Washington on the receipt of his Commission

22   James Innes (d. 1759)

Letter, July 12, 1754, Winchester, Virginia, to the Governor of Pennsylvania, published
in the *Pennsylvania Journal and Weekly Advertiser*
Newspaper
1 p. 15½ x 9¼ in.

Three weeks after George Washington had surrendered Fort Necessity on July 3, 1754, details of the defeat of his Virginia forces in what came to be known as the Battle of Great Meadows began to reach the populated areas of the mid-Atlantic colonies. Col. James Innes of Virginia, commander-in-chief of the forces of the Ohio Expedition, wrote a lengthy letter to the governor of Pennsylvania, James Hamilton, to inform him of the action. The publishers of the *Pennsylvania Journal and Weekly Advertiser* of Philadelphia rushed Innes's letter to press in a special broadside edition of the newspaper on July 25, 1754. Along with the commander's letter, they included the document of capitulation and another letter by an unidentified writer assessing the "disagreeable News of Col. Washington's defeat."

Washington's valiant but hopeless defense of Fort Necessity closely followed his skirmish a month earlier with a French force led by Joseph Coulon de Villiers, sieur de Jumonville, who was killed in the encounter. The French claimed that Jumonville was on a diplomatic mission and that Washington's force of colonials and their Indian allies had ambushed and "assassinated" the Frenchman, allegations Washington later strongly contested.

A scribbled note on the reverse side of this issue of the *Pennsylvania Journal* indicates it was forwarded in a letter of colonial agent Dennys De Berdt (1694?–1770) of London to an unidentified English nobleman in September 1754. In his cover letter (which is also in the Society's collections), De Berdt declared, "I leave to your Excellency to Judge of Washington's conduct." While most Englishmen might acknowledge his valor, they also tended to agree with Horace Walpole's observation that "the volley of a young Virginian in the backwoods of America set the world on fire."

ELS

THE
PENNSYLVANIA JOURNAL
AND
WEEKLY ADVERTISER

NUMB. 607.

THURSDAY, *JULY* 25, 1754.

PHILADELPHIA.

Last Friday came to Town an Express from the back Parts of this Province, by whom we have the Confirmation of Col. Washington's Defeat at the Great Meadows, near the Ohio. The following is a Letter from Col. Innis, who now commands all the Forces on the Ohio Expedition, to his Honour the Governor of this Province.

Honoured SIR,

HAVING Notice of a Person going to your Province immediately, I thought it proper on this Occasion, to give you a short Detail of what hath happened lately.

After having regulated the March and the Transportation of the North-Carolina Regiment, I immediately proceeded to Williamsburgh, and, by my Commission from Governor Dunwiddie, as Commander in Chief of this Expedition, I proceeded to Winchester, where I arrived the 30th of June, in order to take the Command upon me, and to bring up the New-York two Independent Companies, with those of the North-Carolina Regiment, then upon their March from Alexandria for this Town.

Col. Washington with the Virginia Regiment, and Capt. M'Kay with the South-Carolina Independent Company, together, did consist of but Four Hundred Men, of which a good many were sick and out of Order.

On the 3d of July, the French, with about 900 Men, and a considerable Body of Indians, came down upon our Encampment, and continued to fire from all Quarters, from Eleven in the Morning till Night, when the French called out to our People they would give them good Conditions, if they would capitulate; a Copy of which I here inclose you.

After the Capitulation the French demolished the Works; and in some Time after retired to the Ohio, taking two Captains as Hostages along with them. We all know the French are a People that never pay any Regard to Treaties longer than they find them consistent with their Interest: And this Treaty they broke immediately, by letting the Indians demolish and destroy every thing our People had, especially the Doctor's Box, that our Wounded should meet with no Relief. In this Action, it is said, we had about One Hundred killed and wounded, a Third whereof are supposed to be killed. It is reported we killed double the Number of the French. If this does not alarm the neighbouring Governments, nothing can: And I make no Doubt but the French will soon claim this fine Body of Land as their Right by Conquest, if we do not immediately raise a sufficient Force to convince them of the Contrary. What I can learn of their Force, is, that they had Seven Hundred in their first Division, Eight Hundred in the next, and Five Hundred in the last, not as yet joined; which, with their Indians, make a considerable Body.

Col. Washington and Capt. M'Kay told me there were many of our friendly Indians along with the French, sundry of which came up and spoke to them, told them they were their Brothers, and asked them how they did, particularly Susquehannah Jack, and others that distinguished themselves by their Names. It is also reported there were sundry of the Delawares there: We had not one Indian to assist when the Action commenced and ended.

It is my real Opinion that nothing will secure to us the Indians now in our Friendship, if we allow ourselves to be baffled by the French, as it is very natural and common for a more polite People than the Indians to side with the Strongest. So there is a Necessity either to go into the Case in Dispute heartily at once; or to give it up entirely.
I am,

SIR,

Your most obedient,

Winchester, July 12,   humble Servant,

1754.   JAMES INNIS.

CAPITULATION *granted by M.* De Villier, *Captain and Commander of Infantry and Troops of His Most Christian Majesty, to those English Troops actually in the Fort of Necessity, which was built on the Lands of the King's Dominions,* July 3, *at Eight o'Clock at Night,* 1754. viz.

AS our Intentions have never been to trouble the Peace and good Harmony which reigns between the two Princes in Amity, but only to revenge the Assassination which has been done on one of our Officers, Bearer of a Citation, as appears by his Writing; as also to hinder any Establishment on the Lands of the Dominions of the King my Master: Upon these Considerations we are willing to grant Protection or Favour to all the English that are in the said Fort, upon the Conditions hereafter mentioned.

ARTICLE I. We grant the English Commander to retire with all his Garrison, and to return peaceably into his own Country: And promise to hinder his receiving any Insult from us French; and to restrain as much as shall be in our Power the Savages that are with us.

II. It shall be permitted him to go out and carry with him all that belongs to them, except the Artillery, which we keep.

III. That we will allow them the Honours of War, that they march out Drum beating, with a Swivel-gun, being willing to shew them that we treat them as Friends.

IV. That as soon as the Articles are signed by the one Part and the other, they strike the English Colours.

V. That To-morrow, at Break of Day, a Detachment of French shall go to make the Garrison file off, and take Possession of the Fort.

VI. And as the English have few Oxen or Horses, they are free to hide their Effects, and come and search for them when they have met with their Horses; and that they may for this End have Guardians in what Number they please, upon Condition that they will give their Word of Honour not to work upon any Buildings in this Place, or any Part this Side of the Mountain, during a Year, to be accounted from this Day.

VII. And as the English have in their Power an Officer, two Cadets, and most of the Prisoners made in the Assassination of the Sieur De Jamonville, that they promise to send them back with Safeguard to the Fort Du Guerne, situated on the Fine River. And for Surety of this Article, as well as this Treaty, Mr. Jacob Vambram, and Robert Stobo, both Captains, shall be put as Hostages till the Arrival of the Canadians and French above mentioned.

We oblige ourselves on our Side to give an Escort to return in Safety these two Officers, and promise our French in two Months and a half at farthest. A Duplicate being made upon one of the Posts of our Blockade the Day above.

CON. VILLIER.

The following is the Copy of a Letter from a Gentleman at Paxton, about 100 to the Westward of Philadelphia, dated July 16, 1754.

SIR,

I Here met with Robert Calender, who was just arrived from Winchester, and brings the Confirmation of the disagreeable News of Col. Washington's defeat at his Camp at the big Meadows, 64 Miles above Cresaps on the 3d Instant. At Winchester he met Col. Innis, (who now commands the whole Forces on the present Expedition) who had the following Account from Col. Washington; That two Days before the Attack, he had Advice of the march of the French from their Fort by Monagatootha, and made the necessary Preparations for their Reception. The French and Indians marched up within a small Distance of the Camp and beat their Drums in such a manner that Washington judged them to be a good Distance off; and then he beat to Arms: Upon his beating to Arms, the French marched up in sight, and then beat their Drums as usual, and immediately fired, which the English returned very warmly for some Hours. The French then beat a Parley and sent a Summon (a Copy of which is above) to which the English agreed; but no sooner had they delivered up the Camp, than the Indians got in and pilaged them of all their Baggage and Provisions, shot down all their Cows and Horses, and in short took every Thing from them but their Powder, which they destroyed themselves by throwing it in the Ditch that surrounds the Camp; they also killed two of the Wounded and Scalped them, and also three of the Soldiers, who happened to get Drunk and were asleep. Col. Washington upon this complained of the Treatment they receiv'd so contrary to the Conditions agreed on; and the French Commander pretending to put a stop to it, run in among the Indians with his Sword drawn; but instead of persuading them from it, he commended them for their Courage, and the Treatment they had given the English. The Number of the French was 900 and 200 Indians, and what is most severe upon us, is that they were all our own Indians, Shawnesses, Delawares, and Mingo's (or Six Nations) for many of the English knew them, and called to them by their Names to spare their Goods, but all the Answer they got, was calling them the worst Names their Language admits of. The English had but 30 Killed and 50 wounded, of whom 7 are already dead, and no Officer Killed, but one of the Lieutenants of the Carolina Company. The French 'tis thought lost near 200 Men. The English had not one Indian to fight for them; the Half King when he heard of the French being on their march, set off with about 20 Indians to convoy their Women into the Inhabitants; and Andrew Mentour, with the Indians he had with him to watch the Motions of the French, did not come up till after the Engagement. By Col. Washington's Account, there is only about 60 Indians declared in our Favour. While Mr. Callender was at Winchester, a Gentleman arrived there from North-Carolina, and informed Col Innis, that the two Companies who was on their March for Virginia, were Countermanded, the Governor having Advice that a Body of French and Indians, were erecting Forts near the back Inhabitants of that Province. Another Gentleman arrived a little after from the South Branch of Potomack, and informed Col. Innis, that most of the Inhabitants, were coming down to Winchester with their effects, for fear of being cut off by the Indians.

If some Measures are not taken to drive off the French, and by that Means re-establish a Friendship with our Indians, our back Inhabitants must soon be in a miserable Situation.

23 Jacob Nicolas Moreau (1717–1804)

Mémoire Contenant le Précis des Faits, avec Leurs Pieces Justificatives, Pour fervir de Réponse aux Observations envoyées par les Ministres d'Angleterre, dans les Cours de l'Europe

Paris: De l'Imprimerie royale, 1756

vi, 198 pp.

Hailed as "one of the most important documents in American colonial history," this first edition was quickly rendered into English and widely republished under the title *A Memorial, containing A Summary View of Facts, with their Authorities, in answer to the observations sent by the English Ministry to the Courts of Europe.* A compelling propaganda piece intended to counter English claims that French actions precipitated the French and Indian War, its most intriguing feature is a lengthy extract from a journal kept by Col. George Washington.

Marching with four hundred militia to the forks of the Ohio River, Washington encountered a French detachment under the sieur de Jumonville. In the ensuing skirmish, Jumonville and ten of his troops were killed, while another twenty-two were captured. Warned that another French force had taken the forks, Washington fell back to Fort Necessity, little more than a rude stockade surrounded by trenches. Outnumbered nearly ten to one, the Virginians fought for nine hours before surrendering to the French commander, de Villiers, brother to the slain Jumonville. The articles of capitulation permitted Washington's troops to return home unmolested, but the terms also included an acknowledgment that Jumonville had been the victim of an "assassination" while serving as a diplomatic courier. Unable to read French, Washington was unaware of this admission. Moreover, in the confusion that accompanied Fort Necessity's abandonment, Washington left behind his journal. The French easily fashioned this discovery into a telling piece of evidence of Washington's supposed recklessness.

Reading the English translation of Moreau's *Memoire* later, an outraged Washington denounced the "piece, which is called my journal" as "erroneous" and "inconsistent." He went on to complain that "some parts [were] left out, which I remember were entered, and many things added that were never thought of; the names of men and things egregiously miscalled; and the whole of what I saw Englished . . . very incorrect and nonsensical."

RFS

MÉMOIRE

CONTENANT LE
PRÉCIS DES FAITS,

AVEC LEURS

PIECES JUSTIFICATIVES,

Pour servir de Réponse aux *Observations* envoyées par les Ministres d'Angleterre, dans les Cours de l'Europe.

A PARIS,
DE L'IMPRIMERIE ROYALE.

M. DCCLVI.

24   Robert Orme (d. 1781)

Plans Showing the Braddock Expedition and Defeat in the Campaign Against Fort
Duquesne, 1755
[London: Thomas Jefferys, ca. 1758]
6 sheets bound. 9½ x 15 in.

Robert Orme, an officer in the English army who served as aide-de-camp to Gen. Edward Braddock, produced a journal of his experiences during Braddock's ill-fated expedition against Fort Duquesne early in the French and Indian War. Targeting the French stronghold at the confluence of the Monongahela and Allegheny Rivers, the site of present-day Pittsburgh, Braddock marched his combined force of British regulars, colonial militia, and Indian allies through the forests of Maryland, Virginia, and Pennsylvania toward a bloody ambush along the Monongahela. Orme's journal, the original of which is held by the British Library, has long served as one of the key sources on the expedition. His description of one of his fellow aides, George Washington, as acting with "the greatest courage and resolution" during the battle is frequently quoted by biographers.

While compiling his journal, which he eventually presented to the Prince of Wales, Orme prepared (or commissioned) a series of five detailed plans and a map of the route of the expedition. The plans, which clearly reflect the guiding hand of one who was intimately familiar with the scenes depicted, illustrate the line of march, distribution of troops and baggage, configuration of the advanced party, and the field of battle.

Orme's hand-colored, linen-backed plans were long thought to be the work of Thomas Jefferys (d. 1771), a London engraver and publisher. Jefferys had included them in his *Six Plans of the Different Dispositions of the English Army, under the Command of the Late General Braddock* (1758), and later in his *General Topography of North America* (1768). The bound set of plans and map received by the Virginia Historical Society from the Paul Mellon estate appears to consist of remainders that were not used for either of those two publications.

ELS

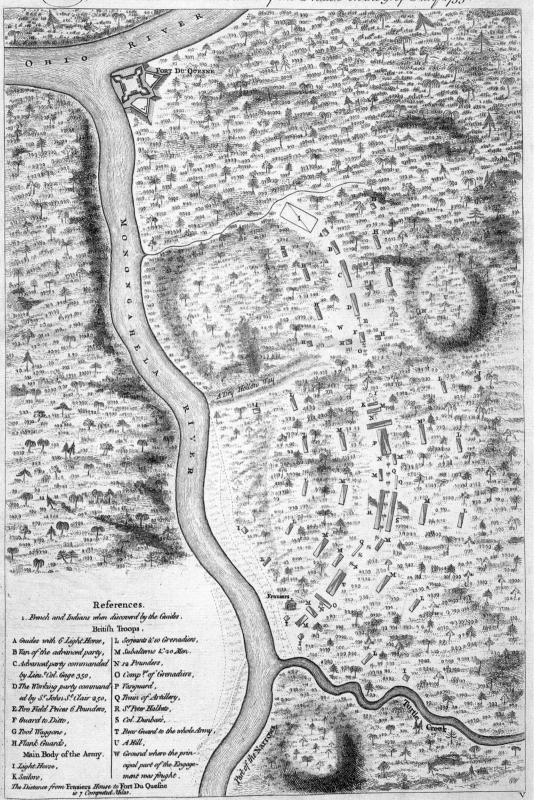

A Plan of the Field of Battle and disposition of the Troops, as they were on the March at the time of the Attack on the 9th of July 1755.

OHIO RIVER

FORT DU QUESNE

MONONGAHELA RIVER

A Dry Hollow Way

Fraziers

Part of the Narrows

Turtle Creek

References.

1. French and Indians when discovered by the Guides.

British Troops.

A Guides with 6 Light Horse,
B Van of the advanced party,
C Advanced party commanded by Lieu.t Col. Gage 350.
D The Working party commanded by S.r John S.t Clair 250.
E Two Field Peices 6 Pounders,
F Guard to Ditto.
G Tool Waggons,
H Flank Guards,

Main Body of the Army.

I Light Horse,
K Sailors,

L Serjeants &c 10 Grenadiers,
M Subalterns & 20 Men.
N 12 Pounders,
O Comp.y of Grenadiers,
P Vanguard,
Q Train of Artillery,
R S.t Peter Halkets,
S Col. Dunbars,
T Rear Guard to the whole Army,
U A Hill,
W Ground where the principal part of the Engagement was fought.

The Distance from Fraziers House to Fort Du Quesne is 7 Computed Miles.

25   Francis Fauquier (1703–1768)

The Speech of the Honourable Francis Fauquier, Esq; His Majesty's Lieutenant-Governour, and Commander in Chief of the Colony and Dominion of Virginia: To the General-Assembly, Summoned to be held at the Capitol, in the City of Williamsburg, on Tuesday the 26th of May, in the 1st Year of the Reign of Lord George III . . .

Williamsburg, Virginia: Joseph Royle, 1761

4 pp.

In the only known separately published copy of this speech delivered in May 1761, Lt. Gov. Francis Fauquier reports on Virginia's role in the French and Indian War (1754–63). Though the war had all but ended in North America by that date, unrest along the frontier kept Col. William Byrd III's Virginia Regiment in the field, involved in the so-called Cherokee War. Prompted by grievances with longtime trading partner South Carolina, in January 1760 Cherokee warriors had attacked white frontier settlements from Georgia to Virginia. In response, the Virginia Regiment was sent to protect the colony's southwestern region. Significantly, the unit did not confine its actions to military matters but constructed eighty miles of road from Chiswell's Fort to the Holston River Valley in North Carolina, a project that helped open the region to Virginia traders.

The speech illustrates attributes that made Fauquier an effective imperial administrator, concerned with balancing the needs of metropolis and colony alike. Rather than emphasizing the military necessity of the regiment remaining on active duty, he suggests that Virginia would derive trade benefits from contact with native peoples. He deftly refrains from dictating to the legislators, telling them that he defers to their judgment to determine "the present State of the Regiment . . . [as] the most competent Judges of the Condition of your own Frontiers. . . ." Ever the loyal imperial functionary, however, he lets it be known that Gen. Jeffery Amherst, commander of British forces in North America, has told him the unit should be kept in the field "until a solid Peace is concluded. . . ."

PAL

THE
SPEECH

OF THE

Honourable *FRANCIS FAUQUIER*, Esq;
His Majesty's Lieutenant-Governour, and Commander in Chief of the Colony and Dominion
of VIRGINIA:

TO THE

GENERAL-ASSEMBLY,

Summoned to be held at the CAPITOL, in the
City of *Williamsburg*, on *Tuesday* the 26th of
May, in the 1st Year of the Reign of our Sovereign Lord GEORGE III. by the Grace of GOD
of *Great-Britain, France* and *Ireland*, King,
Defender of the Faith, &c. and in the Year
of our LORD 1761, and from thence continued
by Prorogation to *Tuesday* the 3d of *November*
following; and then held at the CAPITOL, in
the City of *Williamsburg*; being the First Session of this General-Assembly.

WILLIAMSBURG:
Printed by JOSEPH ROYLE. MDCCLXI.

26 Henry Timberlake (1730–1765)

The Memoirs of Lieut. Henry Timberlake (Who accompanied the Three Cherokee Indians to England in the Year 1762) Containing whatever he observed remarkable, or worthy of public Notice during his Travels to and from that Nation . . .
London: For the Author, 1765
viii, 160 pp.

This book was written as an act of desperation. Its bankrupt author had violated a cardinal rule of government service—never incur travel expenses without written approval or an advance. He had personally financed a visit to London by three Cherokee chiefs. The Governor's Council in Virginia refused to reimburse him, as did officials in London who argued that he went "not by any orders, to the Cherokee nation, but in pursuit of his own profit and pleasure" (p. 146). In hopes of earning money to repay his debts, the young Virginian decided to write a book about his three months among the Cherokees and his taking the chiefs to Europe, but he died on September 30, 1765, shortly before or after publication of his *Memoirs*.

In November 1761 the Cherokees and English made peace on the Long Island of the Holston River. Chief Standing Turkey asked that, as proof of peace, an Englishman accompany him back to the Overhill towns, as those Cherokee villages beyond the Appalachians were called. Ensign Timberlake volunteered. Born in 1730 in Hanover County, Virginia, he had served in the French and Indian War since 1756.

During his three months among the Cherokees, Timberlake noted their cruelty in warfare, their mixed form of government, their relaxed range of religious beliefs, and the impressive architecture of their public buildings and town houses. In his resulting *Memoirs* he also translated a war song, produced an accurate map, praised their food and women, disparaged their craftsmanship, and observed how rapidly they adapted or adopted European ways. Although not infallible, the book is perhaps the best contemporary source about the Cherokees in the eighteenth century. It also was used by the English poet Robert Southey for details of *Madoc*, his epic poem of 1805 about the fictional adventures of a twelfth-century Welsh chieftain who came to America.

JCK

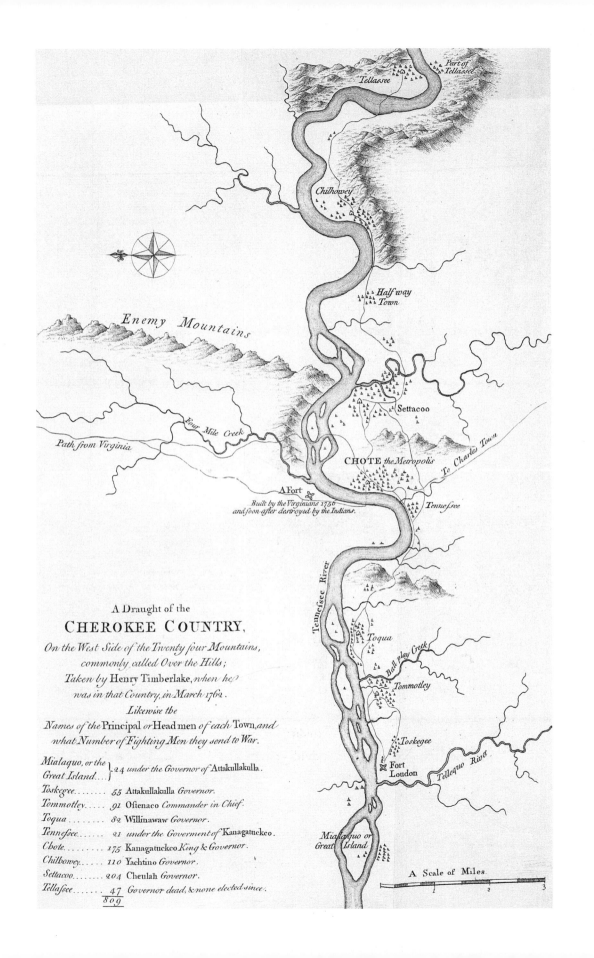

27 "A Lover of His Country" [William Smith (1727–1803)]

An Historical Account of the Expedition Against the Ohio Indians, in the year MDCCLXIV. Under the
Command of Henry Bouquet, Esq. Colonel of Foot, and now Brigadier General in America . . .
London: Re-printed for T. Jefferies, Geographer to his Majesty at Charing Cross, 1766
xviii, 72 pp.

France's defeat in the Seven Years' War created a power vacuum among its Indian allies that boiled into resentment when Britain refused to continue many French imperial practices, such as lavish gift giving. Adding a spark to the volatile situation, a religious movement swept through the Ohio Valley and Great Lakes calling for unity among Native American groups and urging their complete separation from whites.

In April 1763, Ottawa leader Pontiac led a wave of attacks by Indians along the western frontier aimed at destroying white settlements and seizing captives. As part of the British response, Col. Henry Bouquet and fifteen hundred troops were sent to relieve beleaguered Fort Pitt (Pittsburgh) and subdue hostile Indians in the Ohio Valley.

In 1766, William Smith's *An Historical Account of the Expedition against the Ohio Indians* appeared, providing a narrative of Bouquet's expedition. The volume included this image, an engraving after Benjamin West. Bouquet insisted that in return for sparing their villages, Native Americans turn over all captured whites to him, a policy that resulted in considerable anguish for many involved. The combination of word and image in Smith's book makes clear that Native Americans treated captives well, often incorporating them into their own families. He wrote that "Cruel and unmerciful as they are . . . [Indians] exercise virtues which Christians need not blush to imitate. No child is otherwise treated by the persons adopting it than the children of their own body." In a scene full of pathos, a white boy recoils from a British soldier, seeking refuge in the arms of his adopted Indian mother and father, probably the only parents the child remembers.

PAL

B. West inv.

Canot sculp.

The Indians delivering up the English Captives to Colonel Bouquet, near his Camp at the Forks of Muskingum in North America in Nov.r 1764.

28   George Washington (1732–1799)

Letter, December 23, 1772, to William Rind, published in the *Virginia Gazette*
Newspaper
2 pp. 16 x 10¼ in.

Gov. Robert Dinwiddie's proffer in his proclamation of February 19, 1754, of bounty lands in the Ohio Valley in return for service in the Virginia Regiment had long been deferred. The extended course of the French and Indian War, followed by the hostility of Native Americans to settlement beyond the Appalachian Mountains, delayed until 1769 any effort to secure appropriate lands for veterans of the Great Meadows campaign. When that time came, however, their former commander, George Washington, took the lead in procuring a settlement for himself and his comrades.

As colonel of the regiment, Washington was entitled to the largest single proportion of the promised two hundred thousand acres, but he was also clearly moved by paternalistic feelings. He used every effort before the governor and council of Virginia to assure that patents were issued equitably, that each contained a fair portion of the best quality lands available, and that his former soldiers knew how to proceed in acquiring and occupying their lands.

Employing a common eighteenth-century practice, Washington drafted a detailed advertisement in the form of a letter to William Rind, printer of the *Virginia Gazette* in Williamsburg. Ever the stickler for justifying his own actions, the colonel announced that "I have attempted to do [all] in the fullest and plainest manner I am capable of," and "I have now nothing more to do with their land." This apparent attempt to distance himself from future complaints belies the fact that without his tenacious efforts, the promised bounty lands might never have been distributed. Although he acquired extensive tracts of "rich bottom land," Washington himself never realized any significant personal profit from this property.

ELS

THURSDAY, January 14, 1773.   THE   NUMBER 349.

VIRGINIA GAZETTE.

Open to ALL PARTIES, but influenced by NONE.

TREASURY OFFICE, *December* 16, 1772.

I CANNOT sufficiently express my Astonishment that so little Punctuality was observed by many Collectors of the Duties and Taxes, as well as others indebted to the Treasury, in the Payments they ought to have made at the last General Court, and the late Meeting of the Merchants. I know it has been insinuated by some that I am inclined to be over rigorous; but I shall such consider how very essential it is to the Honour of this great Country that the Credit of its public Treasury should be effectually maintained; and let them inform me how I am to answer the Demands of the public Creditors, and be prepared to exchange the Treasury Notes, unless the Duties and Taxes, imposed for these Purposes, are regularly collected and paid.

When I had the Honour of being first appointed to this Office, it is very well known how Matters stood: Many Collectors, largely indebted, were dead, and I found many innocent Securities unhappily involved in the greatest Difficulties. Under these Circumstances I judged it most advisable to reduce Things to Order by Degrees, having Regard to the ultimate Security of the Public. By pursuing this Method I am convinced much has been saved; and I flatter myself it will be found that very few, if any Debts, will be lost which were not desperate before I had any Thing to do with them.

But Indulgencies of every Kind must now be at an End; and my Duty compels me to acquaint all concerned that I shall hold myself indispensably obliged, without Respect of Persons, to put the Laws into the strictest Execution against all such as continue in Arrear after the 25th of *January* next, when another general Meeting of the Merchants is expected; and that I shall, in future, after the End of every General Court, think it necessary to publish an exact List of them, to send me the proper Lists and Copies of the Collectors Bonds, given from Time to Time, that I may be prepared to enforce a Performance of the Conditions of them. I must also request the several HIGH SHERIFFS to make up their Accounts for their whole Counties at once; and, to avoid the Confusion that may be introduced into the Office by the Remissness of many Under Sheriffs, as well as other Collectors, I declare, once for all, that I will receive no partial Payments.

Finding that such Part of the Fund as was expected to arise from Ordinary Licences is likely to be diminished, and it having been represented to me that this is owing to many Ordinary Keepers failing to renew their Licences regularly, I must beg it as a Favour of the Gentlemen Deputy Attornies to give some Attention to this Business, and I will, on Demand, pay all Fees that may arise in such Prosecutions as they may think necessary to engage in, where they cannot be had of the Delinquents.
RO. C. NICHOLAS, Treasurer.

WILLIAMSBURG, *January* 5, 1773.

MR. *Patrick Henry*, junior, of *Hanover*, having been obliging enough to undertake to finish all such Causes of my Clients as remain undetermined in the General Court, I desire that they will be pleased to correspond with, and furnish him with proper Instructions.

As Mr. *Henry* is at a Distance from this Place, I will very gladly do any Thing in my Power towards expediting the Suits, forwarding Subpoenas, &c. between this Time and the succeeding General Court, when I shall deliver all Papers into his Hands, unless directed to the contrary. In most of the Suits still depending I have received a very inconsiderable Part of the Fees, and in many none at all; but if in any Case it should be thought that more has been paid me than my Services deserved, I shall be ready to refund it.
RO. C. NICHOLAS.

RICHARD HUNT SINGLETON, having taken the BRICK HOUSE TAVERN on the Main Street, *Williamsburg*, lately occupied by Mr. *Richard Davis*, returns thanks to all his old customers, and begs a continuance of their favours, as also of those Gentlemen who frequented the above tavern, &c. as he is determined to keep the best of LIQUORS, and endeavour, in every other respect, to give satisfaction.

** Good STABLAGE and PASTURAGE for horses, &c.

MOUNT VERNON, *December* 23, 1772.

Mr. RIND;

PURSUANT to an order of Council, hereunto annexed, I am, through the channel of your Gazette, to inform the officers and soldiers of the first VIRGINIA REGIMENT (those of them I mean who embarked in the service of this colony before it was augmented to a regiment, in the year 1754) that all the claims which had been presented to me, properly attested, for land under Governor *Dinwiddie's* proclamation of the 19th of *February*, 1754, were laid before his Excellency Lord Dunmore, and the Council, on the 31st of *October*, 1771; who thereupon resolved, that each officer should share agreeable to the rank he entered upon the campaign in, and

That	Acres
Each field officer should be allowed	15,000
Each captain	9000
Each subaltern	6000
Each cadet	2500
Each serjeant	600
Each corporal	500
Each private soldier	400

And were pleased moreover to determine that the quantity of 30,000 acres should be set apart for the purposes of answering any claims which might thereafter come in, and for recompencing those who had been, and were like to be, put to any extraordinary expence or trouble in conducting this business.

That about the first of last month Capt. *William Crawford*, who has been legally appointed to survey these lands, produced certificates for 127,899 acres, which he had surveyed in the following tracts, viz.

Acres
51,302
28,627
13,532
10,990
4395
2448
2314
4149
2084
1525
4232
1374
927
127,899

And these surveys being laid before the Council Board on the 6th of the month (*November*) and it then appearing that some of the principal claimants had contributed nothing, and some but partially, towards the several advances which had been voted at the different meetings for the purpose of defraying the expence of exploring, surveying, and other incident charges accruing on these lands, whilst others again had been run to considerable costs and trouble on these accounts, it was thought reasonable and just that every one (the common soldiery excepted) who have their full complement allowed) should receive out of these first surveys in proportion to their advances, leaving those who are deficient in part, or the whole, to be supplied with their respective quantities of land out of the next surveys which are made, towards the completion of which the surveyor has been directed to proceed with all possible dispatch.

Agreeable to these sentiments, on the aforesaid 6th of *November* it was ordered, that the survey of 51,302 acres should be immediately patented in the names of George Muse, Adam Stephen, Andrew Lewis, Peter Hog, John West, John Polson, and Andrew Wagener; whereof, by a regulation approved of in Council,

	Acres
George Muse is entitled to	9073
Adam Stephen, Andrew Lewis, and Peter Hog, to 9000 acres each,	27,000
John West and John Polson to 6000 each,	12,000
Andrew Wagener (whose full claim is 6000 acres, but in this dividend is, by his advances, entitled to no more than)	3428
In all to	51,501
Amount of the survey,	51,302

199 acres short, and to be allowed at the next distribution.

That the survey of 13,532 acres should be immediately patented in the name of George Mercer, he having a claim, on his own account, to

	Acres
	6000
As heir to his brother *John Mercer*,	6000
And for two serjeants, viz. *John Hamilton* and *Mark Hollis*, 600 each,	1200
In all to	13,200
Amount of the survey,	13,532

332 acres too much, and to be accounted for at the next dividend.

That the surveys of 4149 acres, and 1525 acres, should be immediately patented in the name of the heir, or other representative, of Colonel *Joshua Fry*, deceased, who will fall short 832 acres of his proportionate advance, and be entitled at the next distribution to as much as will compleat his quantity to 15,000 acres.

That the surveys of 4232 acres, and 1374 acres, should be immediately patented in the name of Dr. *James Craik*; who will fall short 394 acres of the 6000 he has a right to, and be entitled at the next distribution to that quantity of land.

That the survey of 927 acres should be immediately patented in the name of George Muse, which, added to his allowance of 9073 acres as above, and sale of 5000 as below, compleats his claim of 15,000 acres.

That the surveys of 10,990 acres, 4395 acres, 2448 acres, and 2314 acres, should be immediately patented in the name of George Washington,

	Acres
For his own allowance of	15,000
A purchase from George Muse, as above, of	5000
And for his right to serjeant *Brickner's* share, allowed him,	600
In all	20,600
Amount of the surveys,	20,147

453 acres wanting, and to be allowed at the next distribution.

And that the survey of 28627 acres should be immediately patented in the names of

	Acres
John Savage, who, as a subaltern officer, claims 6000 acres, but by his advances is, at this time, only entitled to	3428

SERJEANTS.

	Acres
Robert Longdon, Robert Tunstall, Edmund Wagener, and *Richard Troller*, 600 acres each,	2400

CORPORALS.

	Acres
Wire Johnson, Hugh McRoy, John Smith, and *Richard Smith*, 500 acres each,	2000

PRIVATES.

	Acres
Charles Smith, Angus McDonald, Nathan Chapman, Joseph Gatewood, James Samuel, Michael Scully, Edward Goodwin, William Baily, Henry Baily, William Coffland, Matthew Doran, John Ramsay, Charles James, Matthew Cox, Marshal Pratt, John Wilson, William Johnston, John Wilson, Nathaniel Barrett, David Gorman, Patrick Galloway, Timothy Conway, Christian Bombgardner, John Houstoun, John Maid, James Ford, William Broughton, William Carnes, Edward Evans, Thomas Moss, Matthew Jones, Philip Gatewood, Hugh Paul, Daniel Staples, William Lowry, James Ludlow, James Lasort, James Gwin, Joshua Jordan, William Jenkins, James Commack, Richard Morris, John Gholson, Robert Jones, William Hogan, John Franklin, John Bishop, George Malcomb, William Coleman, Richard Bolton, John Cincaid, and *George Hurst*, 400 acres each,	20,800
Amount of the claims,	28,628
Number of acres in the survey,	28,627

One acre short.

" And the shares of such of them as are dead, or " have assigned, are to go to those who represent " them, and it is further ordered that the said patents " issue without rights, and with a reservation of quit- " rents from the feast of *St. Michael*, which shall be " next after 15 years from the date thereof re-

29 Robert Stobo (ca. 1727–1772)

Memoirs of Major Robert Stobo, of the Virginia Regiment
London: Printed by J. Skirven, Ratcliff-Highway, 1800
78 pp.

Of all the Virginia heroes to emerge from the struggle between England and France for dominion over the North American continent, none was more celebrated in his own day than the valiant Captain Stobo. This Glasgow native's shrewd business sense and genial personality made him a prosperous merchant in Virginia. Yet when war threatened, he quickly enlisted in the Virginia militia and was with George Washington when the young commander was compelled to yield Fort Necessity to the French on July 3, 1754. Washington's troops were permitted to retire unmolested, but they left Stobo and another officer hostage for the return of two French prisoners. A witness to numerous treaty violations during his captivity, Stobo decided he was no longer honor bound to remain a noncombatant. He therefore made sketches of Fort Duquesne, where he was sequestered, and secretly dispatched them to Washington by Indian courier, along with a letter urging an immediate attack.

When it came, the British offensive under General Braddock proved disastrous. The French discovered Stobo's covert message among the fallen Braddock's personal effects. By the rules of war, a paroled prisoner who broke his pledge was guilty of treason, so Stobo was sentenced to death. King Louis XV stayed the execution. The remainder of the narrative tells of the hero's escape from Quebec in the company of eight of his countrymen as they traveled four hundred miles down the St. Lawrence River to British-held Louisbourg on Prince Edward Island. Having at last reached safety, Stobo immediately returned to Quebec with Gen. James Wolfe, where he reportedly revealed the secret cove that facilitated the glorious English victory on the Plains of Abraham. Stobo returned to a hero's welcome in Virginia, where he had been promoted to major in absentia, and was awarded one thousand pounds "as a Reward for his Zeal to his country."

RFS

MEMOIRS

OF

MAJOR ROBERT STOBO,

OF THE

Virginia Regiment.

ARMA VIRUMQUE.

London:

PRINTED BY J. SKIRVEN, RATCLIFF-HIGHWAY.

M DCCC.

III. *The Westward Movement*

30   John Lederer

The Discoveries of John Lederer, In three several Marches from Virginia, To the West of Carolina, And other parts of the Continent: Begun in March 1669, and ended in September 1670. Together with a General Map of the whole territory which he traversed
London: Printed by J. C. for Samuel Heyrick, at Grays-Inne-gate in Holborn, 1672
27 pp.

John Lederer's writings are an important source for the early history and mapping of the Southeast. Lederer, a German-born physician, led three expeditions to explore the Blue Ridge Mountains and Carolina Piedmont region in the hope of finding an easy route to Asia. (It was a common misconception that the Pacific was only a few days' march from the head of the James River.) Lederer scaled the Appalachian ranges, searching for passes through which traders and settlers might travel. Although he obviously did not see the Pacific Ocean in this area, he did return convinced that he had almost reached it.

After his third "march," he moved to Maryland, where he met Sir William Talbot, secretary of that colony and nephew of its proprietor, Lord Baltimore. Talbot translated Lederer's account from Latin into English and arranged to have the journal published in London. Lederer may or may not have been the first European to reach the Valley of Virginia, but he was the first to publish an account of his discoveries. He was an astute observer of Indian customs and beliefs, and his book was the first scientific report on the western portion of Virginia. His influential map (shown here) provided new data about unknown areas, but it also contained several errors, most notably the "barren Sandy dessert" and a nonexistent lake in North Carolina that were often reproduced by other map makers. Lederer's expeditions inspired other explorers searching for passes through the mountains, and they helped to develop the fur trade with the Catawba and Cherokee.

FSP

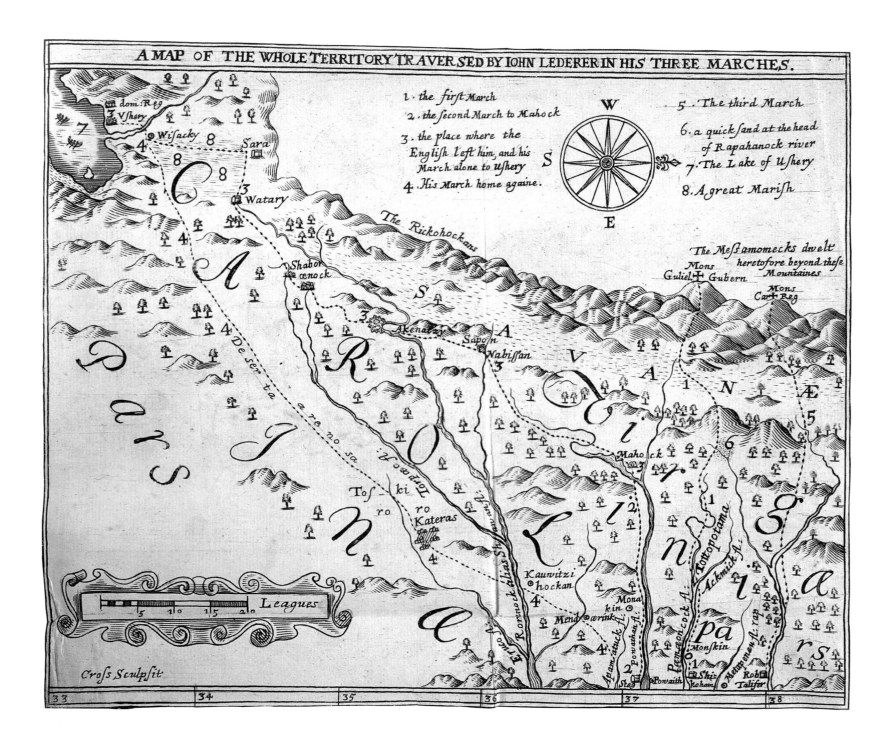

A MAP OF THE WHOLE TERRITORY TRAVERSED BY IOHN LEDERER IN HIS THREE MARCHES.

1. the first March
2. the second March to Mahock
3. the place where the English left him, and his March alone to Ushery
4. His March home againe.

5. The third March
6. a quicksand at the head of Rapahanock river
7. The Lake of Ushery
8. A great Marish

W
S — — E

dom: Reg
Ushery
Wisacky
Sara
Watary
The Rickohockans
Shabor cenock
Akenatzi
Sapon
Nabissan
The Messamomecks dwelt heretofore beyond these Mountaines
Mons Guliel Gubern
Mons Carl Reg
Deserta arenosa
Toskiroro
roKateras
Mahock
Kauwitzi hockan
Monakin
Menderink
Apamatuck A.
Powhatan A.
Pemaoncock A.
Totopotama
Ackmick A.
Metapenensfl. rap.
Monskin
Ste.
Powaith
Ship Kohan
Rob Talifer

Cross Sculpsit

Leagues
5   10   15   20

CAROLINA
VIRGINIA
ers
Pars

33   34   35   36   37   38

31 Samuel Jenner

Neu-gefundenes Eden. Oder: Ausführlicher Bericht von Süd- und Nord-Carolina, Pensilphania, Mary-
land/ & Virginia . . .
Bern: In Truck verfertiget durch Befehl der Helvetischen Societät, 1737
288 pp.

In 1940 an English edition of this volume appeared under the title *William Byrd's Natural History of Virginia;*
or The Newly Discovered Eden. William Byrd II wrote some of the classic texts about early Virginia. Was this another,
previously unknown contribution from his pen, as the editors alleged? In fact, it was not. Instead, it was Samuel
Jenner's wholesale borrowing of *A New Voyage to Carolina*, originally published in London in 1709 by botanist John
Lawson. Jenner took fully half of *Neu-gefundenes Eden* from Lawson, whose own classic text had the sad distinction
of being one of the most-plagiarized early accounts of the American South.

Jenner was a land speculator who wanted to lure settlers to the large tract in Virginia he had purchased
from Byrd. He gambled that he could attract unsuspecting Swiss immigrants by stealing Lawson's account—except for off-putting bits about poisonous snakes and birds that ate up farmers' crops—hinting it was written by
Byrd, and translating the result into German. Jenner's colonization scheme failed, but his literary imposture
fooled the editors of the 1940 translation and misled scholars until Hugh T. Lefler exposed the theft in 1967
(Lefler, "Promotional Literature of the Southern Colonies," *Journal of Southern History* 33 [1967]: 19–20).

NDL

Neu-gefundenes
EDEN.

Oder:
Außführlicher
Bericht

Von Sud- und Nord-
CAROLINA,
PENSILPHANIA,
MARY-Land/ & VIR-
GINIA.

Entworffen durch zwey in dise Pro-
vintzen gemachten Reisen, Reiß-Journal,
und ville Brieffen/ dardurch der gegenwärtige
Zustand diser Länderen warhafftig entdecket/
und dem Nebenmenschen zu gutem an Tag
gelegt wird. Samt beygefügtem

Anhang, oder freye Unterweisung zu dem
verlohrnen/ nun aber wieder gefundenen Lapide
Philosophorum, dardurch man bald zur Ver-
gnügung/ und wahrer Reichthum gelangen kan.

In Truck verfertiget durch Befelch der Helvetischen Societät/ 1737.

32 William Mayo (1684–1744)

A Map of the Northern Neck in Virginia: Situate Betwixt the Rivers Patomack & Rappahanock, According to a Late Survey Drawn in the Year 1737
London: Engrav'd by W. H. Toms, in Union Court, near Hatton-Garden, Holbourn, 1745
1 sheet. 16½ x 18¾ in.

Almost from the date of the grant by Charles II in 1649, the Virginia General Assembly tested the boundaries, if not the very existence, of the Northern Neck Proprietary. All the land between the Potomac and Rappahannock Rivers from the Chesapeake Bay to their headwaters (still unlocated in the early 1730s) constituted a huge territory. When the colony began to issue land patents in the lower Shenandoah Valley, Thomas, the sixth baron Fairfax, protested to His Majesty's Privy Council that this region belonged to him.

The Council ordered a survey of the disputed territory in 1733. A set of commissioners including William Byrd II was appointed to safeguard the crown's interests, while William Fairfax and others represented the proprietor. Byrd hired William Mayo and Robert Brooke to survey the Potomac River, while Fairfax appointed James Thomas, Sr., Benjamin Winslow, and John Savage. Another team undertook the charting of the Rappahannock.

Upon completion of the surveys, the commissioners could not agree on a consolidated map. Each side commenced its own version, Mayo producing his on behalf of the king's representatives, and surveyor John Warner preparing one for Lord Fairfax. Mayo's map, acknowledged as less detailed but the more accurate and visually striking of the two, remained in manuscript form until 1745, the year the Council confirmed Fairfax's title to the Northern Neck.

An English immigrant by way of Barbados and the first surveyor of Goochland County, Mayo had long been associated with William Byrd. The witty colonel had taken him on the famous run of the "dividing line" between Virginia and North Carolina in 1728 and later had him survey the town of Richmond, which Byrd established at the falls of the James River. Perhaps Byrd paid Mayo's chart its most genuine compliment by labeling it "a very elegant Map of the whole Northern Neck."

ELS

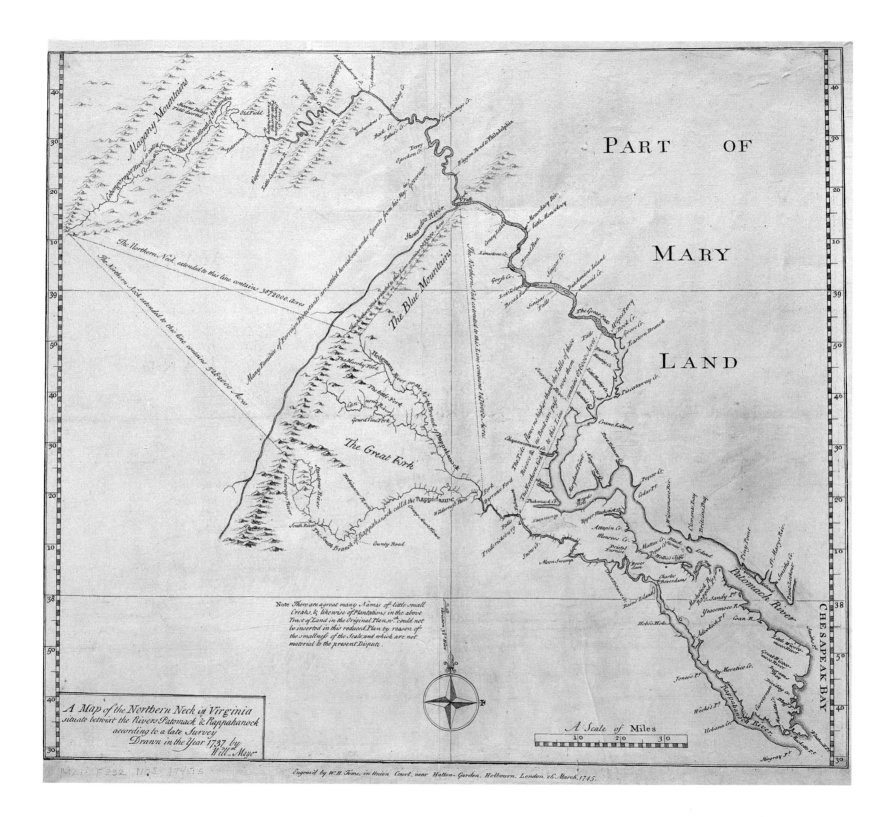

PART OF

MARY

LAND

CHESAPEAK BAY

A Map of the Northern Neck in Virginia
situate betwixt the Rivers Patomack & Rappahanock
according to a late Survey
Drawn in the Year 1737 by
Will.ᵐ Mayo

A Scale of Miles
10   20   30

Engrav'd by W.H. Toms, in Union Court, near Hatton-Garden, Holbourn, London. 26. March. 1745.

Note There are a great many Names of little small
Creaks, & likewise of Plantations in the above
Tract of Land in the Original Plan, w.ᶜʰ could not
be inserted in this reduced Plan by reason of
the smallness of the Scale, and which are not
material to the present Dispute.

33 George Washington (1732–1799)

Survey, April 23, 1751, of 247½ acres in Frederick County, Virginia, for Isaiah Phipps
Manuscript
3 pp. 6 x 7¾ in.

Through his friendship with Thomas, Lord Fairfax, and other Fairfax family members resident in Virginia, seventeen-year-old George Washington secured a commission as surveyor of the newly created Northern Neck county of Culpeper in 1749. With Lord Fairfax's permission, Washington was soon surveying lands in the Northern Neck Proprietary west of the Blue Ridge. By the spring of 1751, when the young man plotted out the boundaries of this piece of land for Isaiah Phipps, he had executed dozens of surveying warrants in what was then Frederick County.

Phipps had paid Lord Fairfax, as proprietor of the Northern Neck, a sum sufficient to secure a warrant for a little more than 247 acres along the Little Cacapon River (what Washington, following local usage, called the Little Cacapehon). The wagon road leading north and west from Winchester toward Fort Cumberland ran through this tract, making it a particularly valuable one, with great potential for development as settlement in the region increased. The site is actually identified on the map of Virginia published by Joshua Fry and Peter Jefferson in 1755 in an area that would later fall into Hampshire County, now part of West Virginia.

Surveys executed by George Washington, with their neatly drawn plats, clearly written descriptions, and examples of the young surveyor's early signature, have always been favorites with collectors. Many of the surviving documents remain in private hands, but this one joins two others from the years 1749–51 now in the Virginia Historical Society's collections.

ELS

Pursuant to a warrant from the Proprietors to
Me directed I have Survey'd for Isaiah Phipps
a certain tract of waste land on the Waggon Road
and upon Little Cacapehon bounded as followeth

Beginning at two white Oaks on ye
S. side the Creek and extended N. 55 W.
One hund.d and eighty pole crossing ye Road
to two red Oaks and a Maple sapling
near a blaz'd chesnut Oak on the side of
a very steep hill thence N. 35 E crossing ye aforsd
s.d Road Two hund.d and twenty pole to
a stake above a marked pine on the side
of a hill thence S. 55 E. 120 pole to ye creek
One hund.d and eighty pole to a white Oak
on ye side of a hill finaly S. 35 W. Two hund.d
and twenty pole to the Begin.g Two hund.d
and forty seven & half acres this 23.d of Ap.l

John Loven 1751   by

John Williams SCC   Washington

34   Joshua Fry (ca. 1700–1754) and Peter Jefferson (1708–1757)

A Map of the Most Inhabited Part of Virginia Containing the Whole Province of Maryland: With Part of Pensilvania, New Jersey and North Carolina Drawn by Joshua Fry and Peter Jefferson in 1751
London: Thomas Jefferys, 1755
1 sheet. 30¾ x 48¾ in.

The renowned collaboration between Joshua Fry and Peter Jefferson commenced at least as early as 1745, when Jefferson was appointed Fry's deputy as surveyor of Albemarle County. During the following year, the two men participated in the survey of the Northern Neck Proprietary, and in 1749 both acted as commissioners for the surveying of the extended boundary line separating Virginia and North Carolina. Responding to instructions from the Lords Commissioners for Trade and Plantations, they produced their most important work in 1751, a manuscript map of "The Inhabited Part of Virginia." Probably in 1754, Thomas Jefferys, "Geographer to His Royal Highness the Prince of Wales," acquired the map, or a copy of it, and published it in London.

Before that date, Fry and Jefferson amended their original map with information received from Christopher Gist, George Washington, and others who had traveled through the Ohio country in the early 1750s. Jefferys consequently issued a second edition of the map in 1755, which now charted the "most" inhabited parts of Virginia and included data supplied by a young captain of the Virginia Regiment, John Dalrymple. The version shown here is the third state of that second edition.

Unquestionably one of the best maps of Virginia produced in the eighteenth century, the Fry-Jefferson collaboration was reissued regularly before 1800 and spawned numerous imitations by other map makers for decades after its first appearance. Its two creators, however, never realized much from their superlative effort. Colonel Fry died in May 1754 after a fall from his horse while commanding Virginia forces against the French. Peter Jefferson, even better known as father of the future president, succeeded to Fry's posts as surveyor, county lieutenant (that is, chief military officer), and burgess for Albemarle County, but he died just two years later in the summer of 1757.

ELS

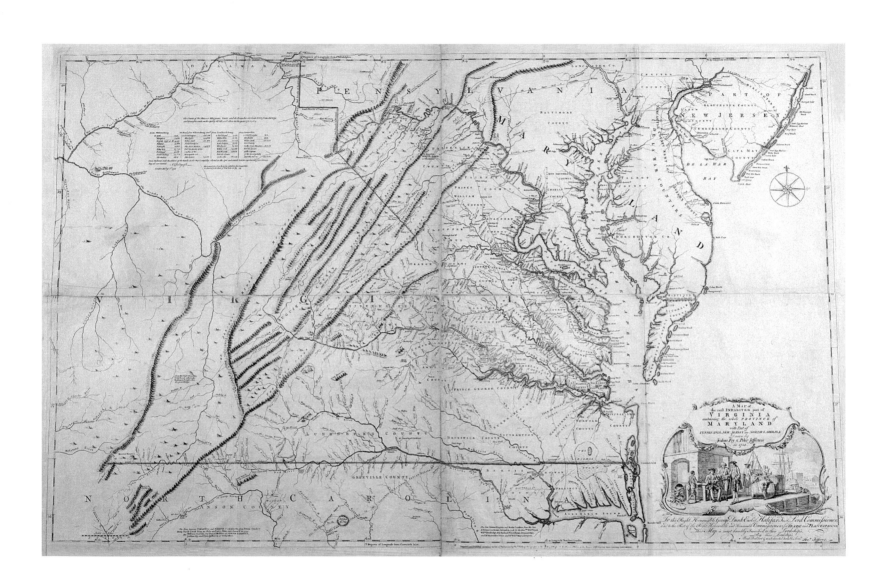

35　John Henry (1704–1773)

A New and Accurate Map of Virginia Wherein Most of the Counties Are Laid Down from Actual Surveys
London: Thomas Jefferys, 1770
4 sheets. 38 x 51½ in. (assembled)

John Henry, Scottish immigrant–turned–Hanover County landholder, surveyor, and sometime school-teacher, commenced his "General Survey of Virginia" in the mid-1760s. He planned to produce a map of the colony that would garner the attention of would-be investors and settlers in Virginia's backcountry, where Henry himself heavily speculated in land.

The resulting map, engraved by the same Thomas Jefferys who had produced the Fry-Jefferson map of Virginia a decade earlier, met with criticism from contemporary map makers (most of whom were his competitors) for being derivative and inaccurate. In fact, most maps of the day relied heavily—and unabashedly—on earlier works. Henry's production, moreover, offered a number of new contributions. The first map to delineate the boundaries of Virginia's counties, it likewise indicated the plantations of major landholders and local leaders. In most counties, the site of the local courthouse is marked with a graphic symbol, suggesting the importance of that structure to the political, legal, social, and economic life of each locality. Finally, Henry's "Concise Account of the Number of Inhabitants, the Trade, Soil and Produce of Virginia" allowed the map's creator to underscore the comparative importance of Virginia among all of Britain's North American possessions.

Financially dependent in his last years on his celebrated son, Patrick, John Henry never realized the fruits of his labor of love. His map, however, remains one of the most valuable visual resources for the study of pre-Revolutionary Virginia.

ELS

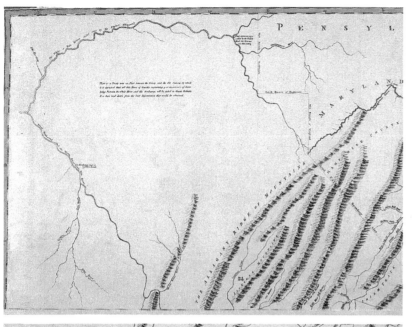

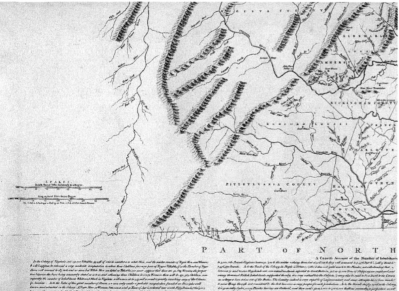

36   Thomas Walpole (1727–1803)

Petition, May 8, 1770, London, England, to King George III
Manuscript
2 pp. 12¼ x 8 in.

In the wake of the French and Indian War and the 1768 treaty with the Indians of the Six Nations at Fort Stanwix, land companies formed with the intent of cashing in on a vast new frontier. Promoted by a diverse group of traders, land speculators, and influential politicians from England and America, one of the more effective of these ventures, although equally unsuccessful in its acquisitive goals, was the Grand Ohio Company, also known variously during its brief existence as the Walpole Company, Indiana Company, or Vandalia Company.

Led by Thomas Walpole, a prestigious banker and member of parliament, the company followed a circuitous route through the British bureaucracy seeking approval for the purchase of some twenty million acres beyond the Appalachian Mountains. Finally, in the spring of 1770, Walpole, joined by his fellow investors Benjamin Franklin, John Sargeant, and Samuel Wharton (1732–1800), was ready to petition the king to proceed with the grant. While the Privy Council pondered this request, tensions in America grew. Within a few years, the cumulative effects of the Boston Tea Party, the continental associations, and the passage of the Coercive Acts had soured the monarch on colonial land companies and doomed the hopes of these bold entrepreneurs.

This petition, a contemporary copy of the original submitted to the king, is part of a significant archive relating to the Grand Ohio Company that was compiled by Sir Matthew Fetherstonhaugh (1715?–1774), a later investor who ultimately poured more money into the venture than did any of the other partners.

ELS

[1770 May 8]

To the King's most excellent Majesty in Council.

The humble Memorial of Thomas Walpole, Benjamin Franklin, John Sargent and Samuel Wharton in behalf of themselves and their Associates.

Sheweth

That your Memorialists and others presented a Petition to your Majesty in Council praying a Grant of Lands in America (Parcel of the Lands purchased by the Government of the Indians) in Consideration of a Price to be paid in Purchase of the same.

That the said Petition was referred by Order of Council to the Lords Commissioners of Trade & Plantations.

That your Memorialists, in pursuance of a Suggestion which arose upon Consideration of said Petition at that Board, of making a Purchase of a large Tract of Land sufficient for a separate Government, were directed to apply to the Lords Commissioners of the Treasury, in respect to the Price to be paid for the purchase of such Tract and the Quit Rent to be reserved thereon.

That your Memorialists in Consequence thereof did on the fourth Day of January last present to the said Lords Commissioners of the Treasury a Memorial & Paper containing a Description as hereto annexed, of the Lands they were desirous of purchasing and for which they offered to pay the

Sum

37A   George Catlin (1796–1872)

Catlin's North American Indian Portfolio. Hunting Scenes and Amusements of the Rocky Mountains and Prairies of America. From Drawings and Notes of the Author, made during Eight Years' Travel amongst Forty-Eight of the Wildest and Most Remote Tribes of Savages in North America
London: Geo. Catlin, Egyptian Hall, Piccadilly, 1844
20 pp. 25 colorplates

Raised in a backwoods region of New York state, "with books reluctantly held in one hand and a rifle or fishing-pole firmly and affectionately grasped in the other," George Catlin was equipped with the training and inclination to visit the Plains Indians of the American West and become, as he put it, their "historian." On observing a delegation of Native Americans in Philadelphia, the artist vowed that he would capture "the living manners, customs, and character of an interesting race of people, who are rapidly passing away from the face of the Earth." He carried to the field two contemporary European philosophies: a belief in the virtue of "natural man" (man living in a natural environment), and a conviction that the scientific recording of natural phenomena was a key to progress. By 1844, when he issued his *Indian Portfolio* of twenty-five plates, Catlin had devoted eight years to the project, had produced several hundred paintings that he exhibited to thousands in America and Europe as his "Indian Gallery," and had written the first of three books about the natives of North and South America. Catlin hoped to publish supplementary volumes of his *Indian Portfolio* that would illustrate additional customs, but the financial failure of the first volume ended the project.

Pictured here is "Buffalo Dance" (lithograph with hand coloring, 12 x 17⅝ in.), which records one of the "Medicine Ceremonies" that Plains Indians conducted prior to a hunting or war excursion. When the herds of buffaloes eluded their hunters, "it [was] decided very gravely that the buffalo-dance must be commenced, 'to make the buffaloes come;' and when such is the case, the dance is kept constantly going, both night and day." The participants wore "masks of the buffalo." When "'buffaloes come,' . . . the dance ceases, and preparations are made for the hunt."

WMSR

37B George Catlin (1796–1872)

Catlin's North American Indian Portfolio. Hunting Scenes and Amusements of the Rocky Mountains and Prairies of America. From Drawings and Notes of the Author, made during Eight Years' Travel amongst Forty-Eight of the Wildest and Most Remote Tribes of Savages in North America
London: Geo. Catlin, Egyptian Hall, Piccadilly, 1844
20 pp. 25 colorplates

To George Catlin the Indians of the American plains were "knights of the forest" who lived "in the honest and elegant simplicity of nature." The prospect of recording their appearance and customs provided him a source of "unceasing excitement." Their hunting of the buffalo became a special interest. As a scientist and natural historian, Catlin recorded the importance of the animal to the Indian. As an adventurer, he was simply thrilled at the sheer excitement of pursuing buffalo on horseback. Catlin wrote that he "tried [the buffalo hunt] in every form."

Regarding the episode pictured here, "Buffalo Hunt. A Surround" (lithograph with hand coloring, 12⅛ x 17⅝ in.), Catlin wrote, "I sat in trembling silence upon my horse, and witnessed this extraordinary scene." He described the episode. "Sixty or seventy young men, all mounted on their wild horses . . . encompassed the grazing herd [of two or three hundred buffaloes] . . . in a circle of a mile or two in diameter." They gradually reduced the perimeter, yelling "in a most frightful manner," as in a cloud of dust they drove "their whizzing arrows or long lances to the hearts of these noble animals." The buffaloes "furiously plunged forward at the sides of their assailants' horses; sometimes goring them to death at a lunge, and putting their dismounted riders to flight for their lives."

In Paris, Catlin's "Indian Gallery" of paintings attracted the attention of critic Charles Baudelaire, who discovered in the artist's colors "an element of mystery which delights me more than I can say." Baudelaire was "intoxicated" with the reds, "the color of blood, the color of life" (shown in the preceding lithograph), and with the "monotonously eternally green" landscapes (shown here).

WMSR

38   Sir Henry James Warre (1819–1898)

Sketches in North America and the Oregon Territory
London: Dickinson & Co., 1848
23 pp. 20 colorplates

The Oregon country had been jointly occupied by American and English settlers since 1818; by the 1840s both nations looked to annex the territory to gain an outlet to the Pacific. Spurred by the interests of the Hudson's Bay Company, the British viewed the Columbia River as the appropriate boundary between Canada and northwest America. Expansionists in the United States looked much farther north and coined the latitudinal slogan "54°40' or Fight!" In 1845, in anticipation that war might break out in Oregon, Capt. Henry James Warre was sent out of Montreal in secret to survey the region. As a British officer, Warre had been trained to sketch the landscape; during the arduous fourteen-month journey by canoe, boat, and horseback, he made more than eighty drawings. By 1846 the crisis had been settled by the Oregon Treaty, which fixed the boundary at the 49th parallel. Warre then converted his sketches and notes into a magnificent colorplate book, the most important one published on the subject of the Pacific Northwest.

Sketches in . . . the Oregon Territory presents sixteen pages of lithographs. Included are dramatic depictions of Puget Sound, Mount Hood, and multiple views of the Columbia River and of the Rocky Mountains. Pictured here is "The Rocky Mountains from the Columbia River Looking N.W." (lithograph with hand coloring, $10\frac{1}{8}$ x $15\frac{11}{16}$ in.). Warre described the Rocky Mountains as "magnificent" and "similar in form to the Alps of Switzerland," but so far removed from settlement that there "you *felt* that you were in the midst of desolation." He noted that the Indians of the region were so reduced in number by disease and warfare that they were a "quiet" and "inoffensive people."

WMSR

THE ROCKY MOUNTAINS FROM THE COLUMBIA RIVER LOOKING N.W.

IV. *Virginians at War*

39   Sir Thomas Gould

Petition, 1677, to King Charles II of England
Manuscript
1 p. 11¾ x 7½ in.

Sir Thomas Gould, a London nobleman and entrepreneur, and his partner, Capt. Thomas Larramar (or Larramore), outfitted the merchant ship *Rebecca* for a voyage to Virginia in 1676. While anchored in the James River, the *Rebecca* was captured by Nathaniel Bacon and his forces during an attack on the tobacco fleet in August. Larramar and his crew were forced to join the rebels, who armed the vessel and went in search of Gov. Sir William Berkeley and his few remaining loyalists, then taking refuge on Virginia's Eastern Shore. In a daring maneuver, Col. Philip Ludwell and a small party of loyalists joined Larramar's English crew in overpowering the rebels on board *Rebecca* on the morning of September 2, capturing the commanders of Bacon's waterborne forces and a significant portion of his troops. Thereafter, the *Rebecca* was commandeered by Governor Berkeley, effectively ending any hope Bacon may have had for controlling the Chesapeake Bay and the major Tidewater tributaries.

The following year, Gould petitioned King Charles II for compensation for the services of his captain and crew, noting that "Larramar and Company behaved themselves with great Loyallty and were particularly Instrumentall in the Suppression of that Rebellion, and Mutiny." Despite the "dayly hazard of their Lives," they had "never received any reward, payment, or satisfaccon whatsoever." On the verso of this petition, an order of the Lords of the Admiralty, signed by their secretary, the famous diarist Samuel Pepys, authorizes a report on the value of the ship and the services of its crew in order to determine compensation.

ELS

To the Kings most Excellent Ma:tie

The humble Peticon of Cap:t Thomas
Gould

Humbly Sheweth

That whereas the shipp Rebecca of London
Cap:t Thomas Larramar having been freighted out on acc:o
of your Peticoner and the said (shipp was in Aug:st 76 forceably entred
and seized rideing at an Anchor in James River by y:e late Rebell
Bacon, and others then Joyned w:th him in actuall Rebellion against yo:r
Sacred Ma:tie in Virginia which they maned & employed in order to the
accomplishing that rebellious designe then on foote. But it happening
that by the Loyalty & valour of the said Cap:t Larramar & the shipps
owne Crew togather with the assistance they received from y:e Governo:r
she was retrived out of the possession of the s:d Bacon, & his accompl:
=ces, Whereupon S:r W:m Berkley yo:r Ma:ts then Governo:r of Virginia
Comanded the said shipp and her Company imediately into the Ma:ts
service wherein she was continnally employed about five months

In all which time the said Cap:t Larramar, and Company behaved
themselves with great Loyalty and were p:rticulerly Instrumenta:ll
in the Suppression of that Rebellion, and Mutiny for w:ch good &
faithfull service neither he nor any of his Ma:ts Company, although
the same was with dayly hazard of their Lives never received any
reward payment or satisfaccon whatsoever, All w:ch appearing as well
by a Comission under the hand of y:e s:d S:r W:m Berkley granted to y:e
said Cap:t Larramar, as by Certificate of y:e Governour, y:e Councell of
State and Burgesses of the Grand Assembly signed by y:e Clerk of the
Assembly hereunto annixed.

Your Peticoner most humbly prays, your Ma:ty will be graciou:s
=ly pleased to take it into your Princely considraccon, That he may
receive such satisfaccon for the use of his Vessell so p:rticulerly
imployed in your Ma:ts service, as to your Ma:ty shall seem most
meet, and to so reasonable a service might reasonably deserve
And yo:r Petico:n: shall ever pray &:c
your Ma:tie

40   Robert Aitken (1734–1802)

"A Correct View of the Late Battle at Charlestown June 17th 1775"
Pennsylvania Magazine, or American Monthly Museum, Volume I (September 1775)
Philadelphia: R. Aitken, 1775
1 sheet. 9¾ x 7¹⁵⁄₁₆ in.

After victories at Lexington and Concord in April 1775, American forces surrounded Boston, trapping Gen. Thomas Gage and his four thousand British troops. Under the orders of Gen. Artemas Ward, the Americans secured two of the heights overlooking the city, Bunker and Breed's Hills on the Charlestown peninsula across the Charles River. On June 17, 1775, Gage sent a force to dislodge them.

This image depicts American forces firing from behind breastworks at the British troops advancing up Breed's Hill, on which most of the fighting took place. At the water's edge is the village of Charlestown (set afire by bombardment from the British warships at anchor in the harbor), and across the Charles River the northern tip of Boston is visible. The bodies shown on the ground convey some of the savagery of the fighting that day. British casualties totaled a staggering 1,150 dead and wounded out of 2,500 troops engaged. Despite inflicting such destruction, the Americans were eventually overwhelmed by numerical superiority, and they retreated to Cambridge, having suffered some 441 casualties.

In September 1775 the monthly *Pennsylvania Magazine* reproduced the copperplate engraving shown here, widely acknowledged to be the first representation of what came to be called the Battle of Bunker Hill. In an era in which newspapers were not illustrated, the publication and circulation of prints such as this and Paul Revere's famous engraving of the Boston Massacre served in no small way to shape American popular consciousness and forge unity among colonists in favor of separation from Britain.

PAL

for the Pena Magaz

A CORRECT VIEW of THE LATE BATTLE AT CHARLESTOWN June 17th 1775.

41   President of the Continental Congress

Letter (Draft), June 27, 1775, to Gov. Jonathan Trumbull of Connecticut
Manuscript
2 pp. 13 x 7¾ in.

     The selection of John Hancock as president of the Second Continental Congress in May 1775 proved to be a wise move. The wealthy Boston merchant lent an air of moderation to the delegates' proceedings while projecting a firm commitment to American rights that emanated from a long involvement in Massachusetts politics. Hancock proved a masterful presiding officer, and when Congress resolved to appoint a commander over the rough assemblage of forces surrounding Boston, he clearly expected to be named to the post. He could barely mask his disappointment when John Adams instead nominated George Washington. The astute Hancock, however, recovered sufficiently the following day, June 16, 1775, to announce graciously the Congress's unanimous choice and request Washington's acceptance of his commission.

     In this unsigned draft of a letter to Gov. Jonathan Trumbull composed a little more than a week later, Hancock lets some of his hurt pride show by announcing the delegates' action but failing to identify the new commander-in-chief by name. That gentleman's identity, his language suggests, could be discovered in the enclosed list of "General Officers over the Forces that are or may be Raised for the Defence of American Liberty."

     Hancock's letter presents an interesting contrast to another communication in the Society's collection. On June 19, 1775, George Washington wrote to his stepson, John Parke Custis, declaring, perhaps somewhat disingenuously, that command of American forces was "an honour I neither sought after, or was by any means fond of accepting, from a consciousness of my own inexperience, and inability to discharge the duties of so important a Trust."

ELS

Philad.a 27 June 1775

Hon.d Sir

By the Unanimous Vote of this
Congress I am directed to Assure you of the high
& gratefull Sense they have of your Wisdom
Assiduity & Zeal in the common cause of these
united Colonies, and to inform you of the
appointment of a Commander in Chief & other
General Officers over the forces that are or may
be raised for the defence of American Liberty,
a List of whom you I have inclos'd the Subordinate
Officers & your Troops to be Recommended by your Assembly or Provincial
Congress to the General, to whom Commissions from
this Congress are sent to be fill'd up agreeable
to such Recommendation —

I am also directed by this Congress
to Acquaint you that by order General
Schuyler is order'd upon an important
Service, in the prosecution of which, they have
Resolved, that if he should have Occasion for a
larger quantity of Ready Money & Ammunition
than he can in convenient time procure from
the provincial Convention of the Colony of New York,
he do in such Case apply to you for such Supplies
of both as can be furnish'd by your Colony, &
you are desir'd to Afford him both Money &
Ammunition, & this Congress will make
provision for Reimbursing the same —

I am also likewise to Inform
you that this Congress have this Day come to a
Resolution that Major Skeene an officer

42   Sir Basil Keith (d. 1777)

Letter, April 20, 1776, Jamaica, to John Murray, Lord Dunmore
Manuscript
4 pp. 9½ x 7¾ in.

     When Sir Basil Keith responded to a letter from his friend, mentor, and fellow Scot John Murray (1732–1809), the fourth earl of Dunmore, his lordship occupied a precarious position. Dunmore had served a tumultuous tenure as governor of the colony of Virginia since 1771, had been ousted from his post, had seen his troops defeated by Virginia forces at the Battle of Great Bridge in December 1775, and now sat with a relative handful of British soldiers, runaway slaves, and loyalists on Tucker's Point near Portsmouth awaiting reinforcements. Keith, in turn, enjoyed a much less threatening situation as governor of Jamaica but still wished fervently that "these deluded fellow Subjects of ours will see their own Errors . . . and that they will return to their Allegiance and the protection of the Parent State under whose sheltering wing they have become such a flourishing people."

     Sir Basil lauded Dunmore's recent "Gallant, & faithful" services to the crown. From the American perspective, those services included theft of the colony's gunpowder supply, at least partial responsibility for the burning of Norfolk, and a disturbing promise of freedom to all slaves who joined the loyal forces. Soon after Dunmore likely received this letter, he was driven from Virginia permanently in the wake of a skirmish at Gwynn's Island. Keith himself lived little more than a year longer, but despite his brief tenure as governor, he kept Jamaica loyal to George III. The islanders, recalling "the happiness they enjoyed under his mild and upright government," later erected a handsome monument to Keith's memory.

ELS

may live to reap the fruits of all your Toils: and
I may live to embrace you and to introduce
My Wife who is sincerely attached to you in
Consideration of the favours & Friendship you
have ever shewn her husband — once more
I leave you to guess more than I have time
to express in the few Minutes Notice I have
of writing to you — If any of my Friends are
with you offer them by best Wishes

    I am ever with the most perfect
    Esteem & sincerest Friendship
    Your most faithful Servant
    Basil Keith

Jamaica April 20th
1776

My dear Lord

    It needs no apology in these times
that I have not sooner answered Your very kind
favour of the 14th of Jan.y which afforded me
the greatest Satisfaction; as it gave me the
Account of your perfect health Notwithstanding
the unremitting cares & fatigues, you are now
involved in — I trust in God these deluded fellow
Subjects of ours will, see their own Errors & the
deceipt practic'd upon them by others before
it is too late; and that they will return
to their allegiance and the protection of the
Parent State under whose sheltering wing
they have become such a flourishing people

    What Merit have You not my dear
Friend; But your Generous Sovereigns
    reward

43 [Baron Friedrich Wilhelm von Steuben (1730–1794)]

Regulations For the Order and Discipline of the Troops of the United States. Part I
Philadelphia: Styner and Cist, 1779
154 pp.

George Washington longed for the day his troops were sufficiently disciplined to stand up to British and German regulars in the open field. A thirty-six page pamphlet, *Rules for the Better Government of the Troops,* was published by John Dunlap in Philadelphia in 1776 but seems to have had little effect. The Continental Army was not long in seeking the service of volunteer foreigners.

Friedrich Wilhelm von Steuben made his availability known to Benjamin Franklin in Paris. The crusty veteran of the Prussian army introduced himself to Washington at Valley Forge in February 1778. He successfully trained a model company of one hundred men in the snow and then extended drill instruction throughout the American ranks to instill the military virtues of order and discipline. Three months later Congress confirmed his appointment as major general and inspector-general of the army. This training manual embodies his ideas and was authorized by Congress on March 29, 1779. Popularly known as the Blue Book, it went through seventy editions, of which this is a first or at least a 1779 edition, and was in use by the army until the War of 1812.

Among the twenty-five chapters are "On the Formation of a Company," "The Manner of Laying out a Camp," and "Of the Treatment of the Sick." Most chapters, however, deal with the manual exercise of arms and what verbal commands should be taught to recruits, or how to maneuver troops. Of eight plates appended at the back, six concern maneuvering, while the others illustrate proper encampments.

Despite being schooled in the harsh discipline of Frederick the Great's army, von Steuben was no martinet. He urged officers to win "obedience through Love and Affection rather than through Fear and Dread." Barely legible writing on the cover of this copy indicates that it initially belonged to "I Company, 3[?] Mas[sachuse]tts Bat[tery], 1779."

JCK

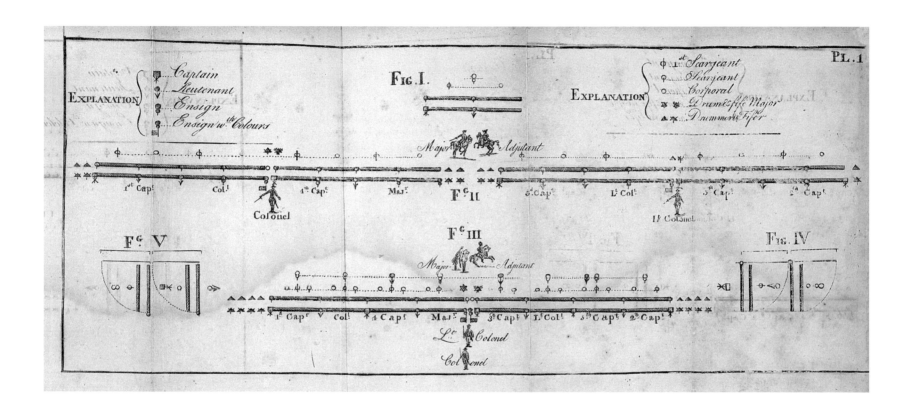

EXPLANATION
{ Captain
Lieutenant
Ensign
Ensign w. th Colours }

FIG. I.

EXPLANATION
{ 1.st Searjeant
2.d Searjeant
Corporal
Drum & fife Major
Drummer & Fifer }

Major Adjutant

1.st Cap.t   Col.l   1.th Cap.t   Maj.r   F.G II   3.d Cap.t   L.t Col.l   5.th Cap.t   2.d Cap.t

Colonel   Lt Colonel

F.G V

F.G III

Major Adjutant

1.st Cap.t   Col.l   4 Cap.t   Maj.r   3.d Capt   L.t Col.l   5.th Capt   2.d Cap.t

Lt Colonel

Colonel

F.G IV

44 Henry Lemoine (1756–1812)

The Kentish Curate; or, The History of Lamuel Lyttleton, a Foundling. Written by Himself
London: Printed for J. Parsons, No. 21, Pater-noster Row, 1786
4 vols.

A curious discovery in the Mellon library, *The Kentish Curate* is a narrative romance written in the manner of Henry Fielding. It was the major work and the only novel written by Lemoine, a member of London's minor literati who supplemented his meager scrivener's income by selling books when he was able, and otherwise acting as a jack of all trades. Though mild by modern standards, *The Kentish Curate* was considered quite bawdy in its own time. The "lubricity of the work is scarcely atoned for by its 'moral' distribution of punishments and rewards," sniffed a later critic who added that Lemoine, though extremely industrious, was "of improvident and too convivial habits."

Lemoine's fictional protagonist, Lamuel Lyttleton, on the other hand, was a paragon of wounded innocence and oft-assailed virtue, an abandoned waif whose search for his natural parents brought him to Virginia during the height of the American Revolution. The only work of fiction among the Mellon collections of Americana, this very rare work doubtless was included for its distantly envisioned, yet surprisingly accurate, descriptions of Richmond, Jamestown, Yorktown, and other Virginia locales.

RFS

THE

KENTISH CURATE;

OR, THE

HISTORY

OF

LAMUEL LYTTLETON,

A

FOUNDLING.

WRITTEN BY HIMSELF.

VOL. I.

LONDON:

PRINTED for J. PARSONS, No. 21, Pater-noster-Row.

M,DCC,LXXXVI.

45 Benjamin Bartholomew (1752–1812)

Diary, May 19, 1781–March 30, 1782
Manuscript
160 pp. 6 x 7¾ in.

Capt. Benjamin Bartholomew, commanding a company of the 5th Pennsylvania Battalion of the U.S. Continental Line, commenced this diary at the start of his unit's march from Reading, Pennsylvania, to Virginia in the late spring of 1781. Gen. George Washington had dispatched the 5th and several other veteran units under Gen. Anthony Wayne to support the marquis de Lafayette against the incursions of raiding British troops in the Old Dominion. Sprinkled with frequent mentions of figures such as Alexander Hamilton, Baron von Steuben, and General Washington himself, Bartholomew's detailed narrative of that long and eventful journey describes the landscape and people he encountered, chronicles the rigors of the march and the ensuing skirmishes between rebels and redcoats, and provides a remarkable eyewitness account of the siege and ultimate surrender of the British army at Yorktown. Bartholomew remained in Virginia with his unit for nearly six months after Cornwallis's surrender, a time that seems anticlimactic to the modern mind but remained tense and uncertain to the people who lived through it.

Eyewitness narratives of the American Revolution, compiled at the time, are decidedly rare, especially regarding the campaigning in Virginia. The author of this unique volume was significantly well placed in the Continental establishment to offer an unparalleled glimpse into both the monotony of the soldier's life and the high drama of the climactic campaign of America's war for independence.

ELS

Miles to Brooks bridge on the
south branch Pamonkey, there enterd
Lousia County 7 miles to Lt Wm Dinie
ds there encamp'd at 8 OClock P.M.
this day march'd 21 Miles, through
a ~~poor~~ Pine Country —

Monday June 11th March'd
9 miles to South Anna Creek
there Join'd the Marquis's and
encamp'd at 11 OClock A.M. in a
Poor Pine Country — This day
march'd 9 Miles —

Thursday June 12th March'd
at 8 OClock A.M. 5 Miles there Halted
to refresh ourselves there 2 miles to

46   **Author unknown**

Glorious News
Providence, October 25, 1781
Three O'Clock, P.M.
Broadside

In early America, information was generally transmitted along well-worn paths, defined by relationships of family and neighborhood, social circle and occupation. The rate at which information flowed was determined by the pace of social interaction, commerce, and printing. Exceptional circumstances altered this pattern; during these situations information raced from person to person and place to place. News of the outbreak of war, the cessation of hostilities, epidemics, conflagrations, and heinous crimes all sped via rumor and report, broadside and newspaper. Certain kinds of news eventually reached nearly everyone, regardless of station or circumstance. Be they Indian attacks in Samuel Sewell's Boston or Robert E. Lee's surrender at Appomattox, eventually news of such dramatic events reached the very corners of America.

This broadside, the only known copy, records the first notice in both Newport and Providence, Rhode Island, of the British surrender at Yorktown some six days earlier. In this instance, the information traveled via the schooner *Adventure*, which departed the York River on October 20, bound for New England. At major cities along the way, Captain Lovett announced the capitulation, spreading the "glorious news" north along the Atlantic coast.

BCG

GLORIOUS NEWS.

PROVIDECE, October 25, 1781.

Three o'Clock, P. M.

THIS MOMENT an EXPRESS arrived at his Honour the Deputy-Governor's, from Col. Christopher Olney, Commandant on Rhode-Island, announcing the important Intelligence of the Surrender of Lord Cornwallis and his Army, an Account of which was printed This Morning at Newport, and is as follows, viz.

Newport, October 25, 1781.

YESTERDAY afternoon arrived in this Harbour Capt. Lovett, of the Schooner Adventure, from York-River, in Chesapeak-Bay (which he left the 20th Instant) and brought us the glorious News of the Surrender of Lord CORNWALLIS and his Army Prisoners of War to the allied Army, under the Command of our illustrious General, and the French Fleet, under the Command of his Excellency the Count de GRASSE.

A Cessation of Arms took Place on Thursday the 18th Instant, in Consequence of Proposals from Lord Cornwallis for a Capitulation. His Lordship proposed a Cessation of Twenty-four Hours, but Two only were granted by His Excellency General WASHINGTON. The Articles were completed the same Day, and the next Day the allied Army took Possession of York-Town.

By this glorious Conquest, NINE THOUSAND of the Enemy, including Seamen, fell into our Hands, with an immense Quantity of Warlike Stores, a forty Gun Ship, a Frigate, an armed Vessel, and about One Hundred Sail of Transports.

PRINTED BY EDWARD E. POWARS, in STATE-STREET.

47   Author unknown

Maps of Actions of the French Fleet Under Command of Admiral de Grasse in 1781
Manuscript volume
9 pp. 7¾ x 12½ in.

A tattered bound volume dating from the late eighteenth century shelters a remarkable set of seventeen skillfully and meticulously drawn maps of naval engagements between French and British squadrons during the climactic year of the American Revolution. Illustrating ship positions before and during the actions depicted, these images appear to be the work of a French naval officer who was apparently an eyewitness to the waterborne encounters.

Nine of the maps show positions of the French fleet under François Joseph Paul, Comte de Grasse, and the British fleet commanded by Adm. Samuel Hood during the Battle of Martinique, April 29–May 1, 1781. A single map illustrates the blockade of the Bay of Courland, which resulted in the fall of the Island of Tobago to the French at the end of May.

The last seven maps depict the Battle of the Capes, September 5, 1781, fought by de Grasse against the British fleet of Adm. Thomas Graves during the siege of Yorktown. De Grasse's defeat of the British relief squadron sealed the fate of the British army under Lord Charles Cornwallis. Included in this set is a map of a portion of Tidewater Virginia (shown here) that features the French blockade of the York River and presents Yorktown, Williamsburg, Gloucester Point, and Hampton in a style reminiscent of the depiction of medieval towns in old English and European maps.

Numerous contemporary maps illustrating the siege of Yorktown and the Battle of the Capes survive in either manuscript or printed versions, but these particular charts do not appear on any lists compiled by modern cartographers.

ELS

48   Author unknown

Ode on the Surrender at Yorktown. To the Honourable William Pitt
London: Printed for J. Bowen, 1782
8 pp.

On November 25, 1781, British prime minister Lord North took the news of Cornwallis's surrender at Yorktown "as he would have a [musket] ball in the breast." The anonymous poet of this piece, however, does not blame the Earl Cornwallis for the capitulation, writing rather that the general "Unnumber'd odds had still defied/But what can valour unsupplied?" (p. 4).

Despite the news, it was not until late March 1782 that North's government fell. The new ministry was led by the marquis of Rockingham. The two secretaries of state were the earl of Shelburne, with jurisdiction over the colonies, and Charles James Fox, with responsibility for foreign affairs. They quarreled, Rockingham died, George III appointed Shelburne prime minister, and Fox resigned. Shelburne negotiated a peace with the American commissioners in Paris, but Parliament rejected it as too generous. Shelburne resigned and was replaced by an unseemly coalition of Lord North and his most inveterate foe, Charles James Fox, who both sacrificed principle to lust for office.

We do not know when in 1782 this poem was written, but clearly its author saw hope for Great Britain's revival coming not from North, Rockingham, Shelburne, or Fox, but from William Pitt, son of William Pitt the Elder (later earl of Chatham), who led Britain to victory in the Seven Years' War.

> Spirit of Chatham! wake, arise!
> Friend of the Isle, and Liberty!
> In bitterness of soul, her cries
> Britannia lifts to Heaven and Thee! (p. 5)

The poet's appeal to the earl of Chatham to send "Thy second self" (p. 6) to rescue Britain was answered. By George III's direct intervention, the Fox-North coalition was sent packing, and in December 1783 twenty-four-year-old William Pitt became prime minister, a post he held uninterrupted until 1801 and again from 1804 until his death in 1806.

JCK

O D E

ON THE

SURRENDER AT YORK-TOWN.

TO THE HONOURABLE

WILLIAM PITT.

Γέμω κακῶν δὴ, κἄκετ᾽ ἔθ᾽ ὅπη, τίθη.　Euripides.

Vix habet in nobis jam nova plaga locum.　Ovid.

LONDON,
PRINTED FOR J. BOWEN, BOOKSELLER, Nº 40, NEW BOND-
STREET; AND AT HIS CIRCULATING LIBRARY ON
THE STEYNE, BRIGHTHELMSTONE.
MDCCLXXXII.

49   **Author unknown**

Recueil D'estampes Représentant Les Différents Événements de la Guerre qui a procuré l'Indépendance aux Etats unis de l'Amérique.
Paris: Chez M. Ponce, Graveur de Msr Compte d'Artois, Rue Ste Hyacinthe, n° 19 / et chez M. Godefroy, Graveur de Sa Majesté Imperiale, Rue des Frances-Bourgois, Port St Michel, 1784
16 plates

    This folio collection of prints, the title of which translates to *A Collection of Engravings Representing the Different Events of the War which Procured the Independence of the United States of America*, illustrates major events in the Revolutionary War from a decidedly French perspective. Of the sixteen steel engravings, eight depict episodes primarily involving French forces, such as the Battles of Senegal, Grenada, Pensacola, Tobago, and St. Eustache, which remind us that the war was also fought in Africa, India, and the Caribbean.

    The engraving shown, "Rendition of the Army of Cornwallis" (plate 10, 15½ x 18⅝ in.), purports to depict the October 19, 1781, surrender of General Cornwallis's eight thousand British soldiers and sailors to the combined American and French forces under Generals Washington and Rochambeau. The printmakers at Monsieur Ponce, without accurate knowledge of Yorktown, could only invent this imagery. They suggest that Cornwallis (at the center) attempted to surrender to Rochambeau (also center, gesturing with right arm), who directs Cornwallis instead to Washington (left, with back to picture plane). In fact, Cornwallis, pleading illness, sent his second-in-command, Gen. Charles O'Hara, to offer the British sword of surrender. O'Hara first offered his sword to Rochambeau, the British officer apparently feeling there was less dishonor in surrendering to the French than to the Americans. Rochambeau declined, directing O'Hara to Washington. Washington refused, as O'Hara was not his equal, and directed the symbol of surrender to his deputy, Maj. Gen. Benjamin Lincoln, who had been forced to surrender to the British at Charleston in 1780.

BCG

Dessiné par le Barbier Peintre du Roi.　　　　　　　　　　　　　　　　　　　　　　　　Gravé par Godefroy de l'Academie Imp.le
　　　　　　　　　　　　　　　　　　　　　　　　　　　　　　　　　　　　　　　et Royale de Vienne &c

REDDITION DE L'ARMÉE DU LORD CORNWALLIS.

8000. Anglais, soldats et matelots, investis à York en Virginie par l'armée combinée des Etats unis de l'Amérique et de France, mettent bas les armes, et se rendent prisonniers de guerre le 19.8bre 1781. abandonnant aux vainqueurs 22 drapeaux, 170 canons et 8 mortiers. Le Charron, vaisseau de 50 canons, une frégate, 2 corvettes et 60 bâtimens de transport, furent pris ou détruits. L'armée victorieuse sous les ordres du G.al Washington et de M.r de Rochambeau, avait pour Officiers généraux M.rs de la Fayette, Lincoln, Struben, de Veiden, M.rs de Viomesnil, de Chatelux, de S.t Simon, de Choisy, de Custine et de Lauzun. dans le nombre des Officiers qui ont trouvé l'occasion de se signaler, on cite M.rs Robert Dillon, Scheldon, Bessroy et Monthurel. Les blessures de M.rs de S. Simon, de Deux Ponts, de Sireuil, de Lameth, Billi, Dillon et du Tertre, leur donnent des droits à la reconnaissance publique

La Capitulation fut rédigée par M.r le Vicomte de Noäilles, le Colonel Laurens, et deux Officiers supérieurs du Lord Cornwallis.

Le 5 7.bre, M.r le Comte de Grasse, commandant la flotte française, ayant sous ses ordres M.rs de Monteil et de Bougainville, avait battu l'Amiral Graves qui venait au secours du Lord Cornwallis. Le vaisseau le Terrible, de 74 canons, fut brûlé; les frégates l'Iris et le Richemond prises. M.rs le Mar.is de Chabert, de Montecler, le C.te de Framond, Capitaines; de Champmartin, de Gouzillon, Capitaines en second; Coyon de Vauroault, l'Hermitte, Maillanne, Destourres, de Krieger, de Hauguen-Houzen, Auvray de la Balaizière, le Cordier, Lieutenans; de Sambucy, de Brochereuil et Dalmas, furent blessés en soutenant l'honneur du pavillon français, ainsi que M.rs Bertrix, Taschereau et Bardin, Off.ers de terre. On regrette M.rs de Boades, Cap.ne de vaisseau, d'Orvault, Rhaab et Villeon, tués.

à Paris, chés M.r Godefroy, rue des Francs bourgeois Porte S.t Michel;　　　　　　A.P.D.R　　　　　　et chés M.r Ponce, Graveur de M.gr le Comte d'Artois, rue Hiacinte.

50   John Churchman

To the American Philosophical Society, This Map of the Peninsula Between Delaware & Chesapeak Bays,
With the Said Bays and Shores Adjacent, Drawn from the Most Accurate Surveys is Humbly Inscribed by
John Churchman
[Philadelphia?: Thomas Dobson, 1786?]
1 sheet. 22½ x 17 in.

John Churchman's detailed and highly accurate map of the Delmarva Peninsula was one of the earliest maps, if not the first, produced and published in the United States. Drafted during the early years of the American Revolution, it features the principal roads, rivers, and streams on the peninsula, along with the shorelines of both the Delaware and Chesapeake Bays and islands, inlets, and shoals throughout the region.

The map appears first to have been issued in 1778. The second state (pictured here) was first advertised for sale in the summer of 1786. This handsome, hand-colored chart can be differentiated from the first issue by the insertion of the word "humbly" in the title and the extension of the Susquehanna River well south of the Maryland border.

Little is known about the map maker or his motivations for producing this work. Possibly, he prepared it for the use of members of the American Philosophical Society who were studying potential canal routes across the peninsula. Churchman utilizes dotted lines to locate several possible courses for the proposed Chesapeake-Delaware Canal.

ELS

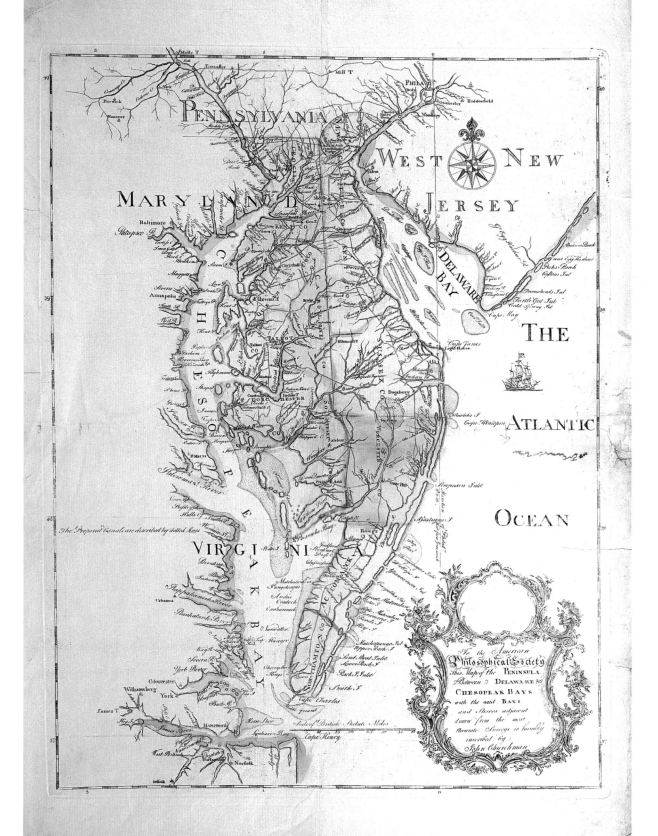

51 George Wilkins Kendall (1809–1867) and Carl Nebel

The War between the United States and Mexico Illustrated, Embracing Pictorial Drawings of all the Principal Conflicts, by Carl Nebel
New York: D. Appleton & Co., Philadelphia: George S. Appleton, 1851
52 pp. 12 lithographic plates

Carl Nebel painted twelve of the most important events of the Mexican War, including this account of Gen. Winfield Scott's entrance into Mexico City ("The Entry of the American Army into the City of Mexico, September 14, 1847"; color lithograph after the painting by Carl Nebel, 16⅞ x 22⅝ in.). George Wilkins Kendall describes the precision and accuracy with which Nebel recorded the landscapes, buildings, and details of each incident, which he rendered at the time of the war.

The lithographic plates are accompanied by Kendall's description of each battle. Reporting the events of the war to the *New Orleans Picayune*, Kendall dispatched first-hand accounts of each incident to the newspaper, later to be compiled in this book.

On the morning of September 14, 1847, the commander in chief of the United States Army, Gen. Winfield Scott, led his troops to the Grand Plaza of Mexico City after a night of intense conflict at the Battle of Chapultepec. Mounted on a white horse, General Scott is said to have ridden through the plaza exclaiming, "My heart is with you," signaling his intent to protect the citizens of Mexico rather than harm them. However, the people of Mexico City, after witnessing the events of the night before in neighboring Chapultepec, were ready to defend their city from the advancing army. In Nebel's painting, riflemen peer over rooftops as they open fire onto Scott's troops while others throw stones from windows. A pedestrian even dares to assault the troops standing nearby. Eventually overcome by the American army, the Mexican citizens yielded to their conquerors as they processed through the square playing "Yankee Doodle" and other patriotic songs. In the distance, the American flag rises on the staff above the National Palace, signifying the victory of Scott's troops over Mexico City. Their entry into the city marked the last major conflict of the 1846 Mexican War, which was finally resolved by a peace treaty in February 1848.

ACd

52A   A[lfred] W[ordsworth] Thompson (1840–1896)

"Irregular Troops of Virginia. Riflemen of the Alleganies," 1861
Pencil and ink on paper. 9½ x 7 in.

Born in Baltimore, Alfred Wordsworth Thompson initially studied law in his father's office but before the outbreak of the Civil War decided to become a painter. At the time of John Brown's raid, Thompson traveled to Harpers Ferry and made drawings of the site of the raid, as well as a likeness of Brown, whom he visited in prison. Upon the outbreak of hostilities, Thompson worked as a war illustrator, and many of his pictures appeared in *Harper's Weekly* and the *Illustrated London News*. In 1861, Thompson went to France for further study, where he remained through the year 1868. Upon his return to America, the artist opened a studio in New York City, where he became a well-known landscape and historical painter.

Drawings of the war from the Confederate side are extremely rare; among the few other examples are the work of Frank Vizetelly for the *Illustrated London News*. This drawing captures one outcome of early efforts to create an army out of those who rushed to enlist in the Confederate States of America's forces in 1861. These Confederates gathering in the Shenandoah Valley may be volunteering for service or may have already been mustered in. At this early date, Confederate uniforms were not yet standardized; enlistees wore their own clothing or any local militia uniforms they might have owned. Nor had the CSA yet standardized its weapons. Visible are a hatchet and several distinct types of pistols, as well as a variety of rifles and muskets. In time, uniforms and weaponry would be standardized, and a powerful army created from these inauspicious beginnings.

BCG

Irregular Troops of Virginia. "Riflemen of the Alleganies"

1/2 Page

52B   A[lfred] W[ordsworth] Thompson (1840–1896)

"Market Place in Winchester, Va. Rendezvous of the Militia of the lower Valley of the Shenandoah," 1861
Pencil and ink on paper. 12¼ x 9⅝ in.

Market houses stood at the center of Virginia's nineteenth-century incorporated towns, the most important civic structures in those early municipalities. Politically, the market house (through the courts and council chambers sometimes housed within) symbolized the emerging importance of towns as the landscape of Virginia became more densely populated, and as cities began to challenge the economic, political, and social hegemony of the agrarian countryside.

Winchester, the largest city in the Shenandoah Valley at the outbreak of hostilities in 1861, had a market house in place as early as 1770. It served thereafter as the city center, in this case, as a rallying point for troops mustering in the army of the Confederate States of America. This Alfred Wordsworth Thompson drawing depicts troops parading in the market yard, as well as troops—apparently only just mustered in—that are not yet similarly equipped. In place of uniform jackets, several plaid shirts are visible. Many of these troops were initially stationed in Winchester and came under the command of Thomas Jonathan Jackson, who left the Virginia Military Institute and by April 1861 commanded Confederate troops in Harpers Ferry, but had not yet earned the sobriquet "Stonewall."

BCG

52C   A[lfred] W[ordsworth] Thompson (1840–1896)

"A Family of Virginians leaving their Home and going South on the advance of Genl
Patterson's army from Martinsburg," 1861
Pencil, ink, and watercolor wash on paper. 12⅝ x 9½ in.

       Union general Robert Patterson was in command of the Department of Pennsylvania, which also included Delaware and part of Maryland. Patterson, who had never before held independent command, first faced Confederates at Harpers Ferry under Col. Thomas J. Jackson (soon replaced by Gen. Joseph E. Johnston) and then devised a plan to capture Harpers Ferry and move into Virginia. For a time, it looked as though Patterson might succeed. In the face of his advance, refugees streamed south. Alfred Wordsworth Thompson drew a family fleeing Patterson's advance and wrote of what he saw:

> On the advance of Genl. Patterson in the direction of Winchester. Many Wealthy families
> of Berkeley, Clark, & Jefferson Counties who from their Secession proclivities considered
> it unsafe to remain at home, deserted their farms and plantations taking their Servants and
> such articles of Comfort as could be conveniently carried, and moved off up the Valley,
> beyond Woodstock or Harrisonburg. For some days after Genl. Johnson fell back on Winchester numbers of Carriages could be seen containing the female portion of a family, the
> Master of the House riding in advance with fowling piece or rifle slung to his back, such
> of the woman servants not left behind to take care of the property being sent ahead in a
> Wagon, the Males marching beside the Carriage each armed with a gun, as they say, 'to
> keep de d——Yankees and abumlishioners from harmin de Ladies.'

BCG

½ page

A Family of Virginians leaving their Home and going South in the advance of Genl Patterson's Army from Martinsburg

53 Thomas Place (b. 1839?)

"War Reminiscences of Thomas Place," compiled ca. 1900
Manuscript volume
44 pp. 11¼ x 13¾ in.

This extraordinary scrapbook-memoir was compiled by a Hempstead, New York, native who enlisted in the Union Army in September 1862 and joined Troop H of the 1st New York Mounted Rifles at the siege of Suffolk, Virginia. Place included in this volume photographs of himself and other members of his unit, records concerning his own military service, and an extensive series of pencil sketches and hand drawings of an exceptional variety of scenes and events associated with campaigns around Suffolk and on the peninsula.

The bulk of Place's primitive but highly interesting sketches, presumably drawn while he was in military service, document the Suffolk Campaign and the lower Tidewater region. They include images of army camps and fortifications, scenes of camp life and military clashes, and views of churches, plantation homes, and villages. Several drawings depict local African Americans in revealing, though often stereotypical, fashion. Later sketches include views of the Dismal Swamp, Williamsburg, a slave community at Gloucester Point, and the Bermuda Hundred Campaign.

Visual representations of the siege of Suffolk in any format are comparatively rare. This volume presents a singular perspective on that campaign and on the country surrounding that beleaguered town. It serves as a remarkable visual record of one man's experiences, both the mundane and the harrowing, in Civil War–era Virginia.

ELS

Death of Lieut Disosway, of Troop M. at Williamsburg, Va. Oct 14ᵗʰ 1863 (Acting Provo Marshal) shot by John Boyle of Troop H. while intoxicated.

Williamsburg Va. the main street, courthouse of two counties on either side, one on the right used a picket station, built of brick brought from England, and where Patrick Henry, said, "Give me liberty, or give me death"

54A   Winslow Homer (1836–1910)

Campaign Sketches
Boston: L. Prang & Co., 1863
7 plates plus title page

In 1861 and 1862 the magazine *Harper's Weekly* sent illustrator Winslow Homer to Virginia to cover the Civil War. There the aspiring painter, age twenty-five and with plans to study in Europe, found art training of a different sort. With the Army of the Potomac, first outside Washington and then during the Peninsular Campaign directed against Richmond, Homer made sketches, primarily of camp life. From these were derived wood engravings that appeared in *Harper's*, oil paintings, and lithographs. Homer reserved his most profound thoughts about the war for the medium of oil, but even there he sometimes pursued the humor instead of the tragedy of army life. Humor is prominent in four of Homer's six *Campaign Sketches*. In all of this imagery, the artist recognized the democratic nature of the new American war by focusing on ordinary individuals, not on the martial pageantry of the past.

Pictured here is "Foraging" (lithograph, 14 x 11 in.). Three soldiers anxious to supplement meager army rations have attempted to "take a bull by the horns." Instead, they are unable to subdue an immense animal that now seems to threaten even the viewer, placing all "on the horns of a dilemma." In the background an officer looks the other way. A black man who waves his arms in consternation is a comical and ambiguous figure, either the former owner of the beast, the slave of its owner, or a concerned accomplice. Following the war, Homer would take a decidedly more sympathetic position regarding African Americans, painting some of the era's most sensitive depictions of them.

WMSR

FORAGING.

LITH. & PUB. BY L. PRANG & Cº BOSTON, MASS.

54B   Winslow Homer (1836–1910)

Campaign Sketches
Boston: L. Prang & Co., 1863
7 plates plus title page

Winslow Homer's *Campaign Sketches* stands as a landmark in his career as a printmaker. Unlike his illustrations that since 1857 had appeared in such magazines as *Ballou's Pictorial* and *Harper's Weekly*, these images were conceived to stand independently. Unlike those earlier wood engravings, which were in part the work of intermediaries who routinely altered imagery as they prepared it for publication, the *Campaign Sketches* were transferred to the lithographic stone by Homer himself. These were published by Louis Prang to answer the interest of northerners in the progress of the war. They failed, however, to sell. The six lithographs (seven with the title page) were "Part I" of a projected series that was never continued. Today the plates are extremely rare. Paul Mellon's set contains all seven plates and is unique in that each print is signed by the artist. This set probably was a proof edition.

While resident with the Army of the Potomac in Virginia, Homer made several drawings of black teamsters who handled the mules and horses that pulled the supply wagons of Gen. George McClellan's force. One of the drawings became the *Campaign Sketch* pictured here, "The Baggage Train" (lithograph, 14 x 11 in.), an image that is both humorous and thoughtful. Two teamsters hitch a ride and avoid the mud of the road. The figure to the right wears two left shoes. The raised whip in the background and the sinking wheels of the wagon suggest that its progress is mired by its extra baggage of human cargo. Whether such contrabands—the African Americans who served the Union army in various noncombat roles—pulled their own weight was a subject of debate at the time in the northern press.

WMSR

THE BAGGAGE TRAIN.

LITH. & PUB. BY L. PRANG & Cº BOSTON, MASS.

V. Virginians at Work

55 James I (1566–1625)

A Counterblaste to Tobacco
London: R. Barker, 1604
25 pp.

Tobacco was first imported into Spain and Portugal in the early sixteenth century, and it immediately generated fierce controversy. Early proponents in England praised its medicinal benefits, but others condemned it as a "heathen fume." One of its most scathing critics was James I, who reputedly became ill after his first attempt at smoking. The king warned his subjects in this tract that smoking led to depravity and stated that it is "a custom loathsome to the eye—hateful to the nose—harmful to the brain—dangerous to the lungs—and, in the black stinking fumes therof, nearest resembling the horrid Stygian fumes of the pit that is bottomless."

Although published anonymously, the authorship of *Counterblaste* was an open secret, and it became one of the best known of the tobacco tracts. James's warnings were ignored, and the use of tobacco increased rapidly during his reign. Nine years after the publication of *Counterblaste*, John Rolfe exported the first shipment of Virginia-grown tobacco to England. London merchants were immediately enthusiastic and offered to buy as much tobacco as Jamestown could produce. Virginia exported twenty thousand pounds of tobacco in 1617 and twice that amount the following year. When the royal coffers began to fill up from the taxes and duties levied on this crop, the king's criticisms of this "filthy novelty" eased.

FSP

A
COVNTER-
BLASTE TO
Tobacco.

¶ Imprinted at London
by R. B.
Anno 1604.

56 John Deacon (fl. 1585–1616)

Tobacco Tortured, or, The Filthie Fume of Tobacco Refined: Shewing all sorts of Subjects, that the Inward taking of Tobacco Fumes, is very Pernicious unto Their Bodies . . .
London: Printed by Richard Field dwelling in Great Woodstreete, 1616
197 pp.

In the sixteenth century, tobacco was hailed by some as the greatest medical curative, "the divine herb." Others blamed tobacco for causing some three hundred diseases, among them syphilis, smallpox, and cancer. This debate over the benefits of tobacco generated an extensive series of pamphlets. One of the anti-tobacconists was the fanatic John Deacon, who dedicated his tract to King James I, the most famous propagandist in the campaign against tobacco.

Tobacco Tortured was written as a dialogue between two speakers, the youthful Capnistus and Hydrophorus (the author). Capnistus planned to import tobacco from the West Indies, and Hydrophorus earnestly tried to convince him of the evils of "the intoxicating filthie fumes of Tobacco." Deacon divided the work into two parts, the first arguing the health risks associated with tobacco smoke, and the second warning of the economic consequences of the trade to the "publike state." Written in a florid and almost hysterical style and crammed with Biblical quotations, *Tobacco Tortured* prompted one critic to call this work the "most naively absurd anti-tobacco tract ever produced."

FSP

TOBACCO
TORTVRED,
OR,
THE FILTHIE FVME OF
TOBACCO REFINED:

shewing all sorts of Subiects, that the inward taking of
Tobacco *fumes, is very pernicious vnto their bodies; too*
too profluuious for many of their purses; and most pestife-
rous to the publike State. Exemplified appa-
rently by most fearefull effects:

More especially, from their treacherous proiects about the
Gun-powder Treason; From their rebellious attempts of
late, about their preposterous disparking of certaine
Inclosures: as also, from sundry other
their prodigious practises.

Prov. 27. 9.

If sweete oyntments and perfumes do vndoubtedly reioyce the heart of a man: then
surely, all noysome sauours, and poysonsome smels (such as is the filthie
fume of Tobacco) inwardly taken, must necessarily disquiet,
and driue the same into a dangerous condition.

Dignitatis Διάκονος *Deus.*

LONDON,
Printed by RICHARD FIELD dwelling in Great
Woodstreete. 1616.

57   Charles I (1600–1649)

By the King. A Proclamation Concerning Tobacco
London: Imprinted at London by Robert Barker, Printer to the Kings Most Excellent
Maiestie and by the Assignes of John Bill, 1630
Broadside

Royal proclamations once constituted the English law of the land. By the time Charles I issued this broadside bearing his royal coat of arms, proclamations had become more a declaration of the monarch's will. The right of the monarch to grant exclusive power to individuals to engage in trade in return for fees paid to the crown, however, remained unquestioned. During the early 1600s most of the proclamations directed to the American colonies dealt with the tobacco trade.

Many of the colonists in Virginia made their fortune in tobacco, and their wealth rose and fell with its price. The planters opposed duties levied upon the crop, but England derived important revenue while at the same time opposing the development of a one-crop economy. These competing interests came to a head in the years 1630–31 with the proclamation of January 6. In it the king forbade the growing of tobacco in the British Isles and restricted the importation of all tobacco except that grown in the English colonies in Virginia and certain Caribbean islands. The proclamation required strict inspection regulations, and King Charles predicted that the plantations "lingering onely upon Tobacco, are in apparent danger to be utterly ruined." Despite this warning and a system of stringent controls, the colonists continued to pin their fortunes on this one crop. The plant thrived in the Virginia soil and climate, and it could be produced in greater quantities per acre than other crops. Tobacco became the money crop of Virginia, even serving as currency during much of the colonial period.

FSP

⊰ By the King.

¶ A Proclamation concerning Tobacco.

Hereas in the Reigne of Our moſt deare and Royall Father, King I A M E S of bleſſed memory, ⅋ ſince Our acceſſe to the Crowne, ſeuerall Proclamations haue been made and publiſhed concerning Tobacco, Yet notwithſtanding all the care and prouidence which hath hitherto been vſed, We finde the vnlimited deſire of gaine, and the inordinate appetite of taking Tobacco, hath ſo farre preuailed, that Tobacco hath been continued to bee planted in great quantities, in ſeuerall parts of this Our Realme, and a vaſt proportion of vnſeruiceable Tobacco made and brought from Our Colonies of Virginia, Summer Ilands, and other Our Forreigne Plantations, beſides an incredible quantity of Braſill and Spaniſh Tobacco imported hither, and ſecretly conueyed on Land. And it is now come to paſſe, That thoſe Our Forreigne Plantations, that might become vſefull to this Kingdome, lingering onely vpon Tobacco, are in apparant danger to be vtterly ruined, vnleſſe Wee ſpeedily prouide for their ſubſiſtence; The bodies and manners of Our people are alſo in danger to bee corrupted, and the wealth of this Kingdome exhauſted by ſo vſeleſſe a weede as Tobacco is; which beeing repreſented vnto Us by the humble Petition of Our louing Subiects the Planters and Aduenturers in Virginia, and alſo by the like humble Petition of the Retailers and Sellers of Tobacco in and about Our Cities of London and Weſtminſter, Wee haue thought it worthy of Our Princely care, as a matter not only fit for Our profit, ⅋ the profit of Our people, but much concerning Us in Our honour and gouernment ſo to regulate the ſame, and compell due obedience thereto, that Our Forreigne Plantations and Colonies may bee ſupported and encouraged, and they made vſefull to this Kingdome, by applying themſelues to more ſolide commodities, that the healths of Our Subiects may be preſerued, the wealth of this Kingdome enlarged, and the manners of Our people ſo ordered and gouerned, that the world may not iuſtly taxe Us, that theſe are at once endangered only by the licentious vſe of Tobacco. And therfore hauing ſeriouſly aduiſed hereof, Wee, by the aduice of Our Priuie Councell, haue now reſolued vpon, and publiſhed theſe Our Commands following concerning Tobacco, which Our Royall will and pleaſure is, ſhall be in all things obſerued vpon paine of Our higheſt diſpleaſure, and of ſuch paines, penalties and puniſhments, as by Our Court of Exchequer, and Court of Starre Chamber, and by any other Courts and miniſters of Iuſtice, or by Our Prerogatiue Royall can be inflicted vpon the offendors.

58 Edward Williams (fl. 1650)

Virginia: more especially the South part thereof, Richly and truly valued . . . The Second Edition, with Addition of The Discovery of Silkworms, with their benefit. And Implanting of Mulberry Trees . . .
London: Printed by T. H. for John Stephenson, at the Sign of the Sun below Ludgate, 1650
2 parts in one vol.

When the leaders of the Virginia Company of London backed the new colony, they hoped the return on their investment would be in gold, furs, iron, glass, timber, and silk. James I championed the silk industry in England and ordered the planting of tens of thousands of mulberry trees, the essential food for silkworms. These attempts were not commercially successful, however, and he then encouraged his countrymen to export the endeavor to Virginia, where there was an abundance of native mulberry trees. Books and pamphlets of instruction were sent to the colonists, the most important of these being *Virginia's Discovery of Silke-Wormes*, written by Edward Williams and first published in London in 1650, and bound here with *Virginia: more especially the South part thereof, Richly and truly valued.*

Williams's work revealed the European fascination with the silk market and the desire to find a domestic source for this exotic luxury. He instructed the new colonists to grow silk so that "wee shall be free from the imperious usurpations of forraigne Princes upon your estates" and concluded by stating that "By these noble undertakings wee contract China two thousand Leagues nearer to us." Governors Edward Digges and Sir William Berkeley promoted Virginia sericulture, but despite their efforts, there was never enough skilled labor to make silk production profitable. Most planters showed little interest in raising silk, and by the end of the 1600s tobacco remained king.

FSP

VIRGINIA:

More especially the South part thereof, Richly and truly valued: *viz.*

The fertile *Carolana,* and no lesse excellent Isle of *Roanoak,* of Latitude from 31. to 37. Degr. relating the meanes of raysing infinite profits to the Adventurers and Planters.

The second Edition, with Addition of

THE DISCOVERY OF SILKWORMS, with their benefit.

And Implanting of Mulberry Trees.

ALSO

The Dressing of Vines, for the rich Trade of making Wines in VIRGINIA.

Together with

The making of the Saw-mill, very usefull in *Virginia,* for cutting of Timber and Clapbord to build withall, and its Conversion to many as profitable Uses.

By *E. W.* Gent.

LONDON,

Printed by *T. H.* for *John Stephenson,* at the Sign of the Sun below Ludgate. 1650.

This Figure pourtraies the Cods, with the Butterflies come forth of them, to lay their Egges upon black Serge, Chamlet, Tammy, or such like stuffe, as in this Treatise is shewed.

59   **Thomas Boreman**

A Compendious Account of the Whole Art of Breeding, Nursing, and the Right Ordering of the Silk-worm.
Illustrated with Figures engraven on Copper: Whereon is curiously exhibited the whole Management of this
Profitable Insect
London: Printed for J. Worrall, at the Dove in Bell-Yard, near Lincolns-Inn; Olive Payne,
in Round Court in the Strand; Thomas Boreman, on Ludgate-Hill, 1733
32 pp.

    The first interest in silk culture in colonial America stemmed from the discovery of native mulberry trees growing in Virginia. King James I, seeking a way to avoid the heavy importation charges, promoted the development of sericulture in Virginia and sent the colonists detailed instructions and materials for silk cultivation. The attempt was not successful, but it did not discourage other colonies from undertaking this unfamiliar and labor-intensive process. Silk culture was one of the main considerations in the settlement of Georgia, and Thomas Boreman dedicates his *Compendious Account* to the "trustees for establishing the colony of Georgia in America."

    Boreman's instructions described the more elaborate methods then used in European silk-making. There, moths laid their eggs on cloth (not trees), and the worms were then gathered and fed on shelves of mulberry leaves, as shown in this plate. After the worms spun the cocoons, the cases were gathered, and the silken fiber of the cocoon was spun into thread. Two years after the publication of this book, Georgia exported eight pounds of silk; in 1759, more than one thousand pounds left the colony. Although advocates of Georgia predicted that it would be an ideal place for the silk culture to thrive, the lack of skilled labor thwarted the dream of huge savings on silk imports.

FSP

Plate IV. Page 18.

In this Draught is ſhewn how you are to range your Scaffold and Shelves to place your Worms, and Leaves to feed them.

60   John Epperson

Map of Appomattox River West of Petersburg, Va., July 15, 1797
Manuscript map
2 sheets. 13¼ x 33¼ in. (assembled)

Beginning in 1787, the Virginia General Assembly passed a series of acts authorizing "the clearing, improving, and extending the navigation of Appamattax river, to the highest part practicable," an enterprise deemed "of great benefit and public utility." The assembly's efforts culminated in 1795 with the act creating the Upper Appomattox Company, whose trustees were empowered to initiate projects that would ensure "a sufficient depth and width of water to navigate boats, batteaus or canoes capable of carrying eight hogsheads of tobacco."

Along with deepening and widening the river at certain points, the trustees were likewise authorized "in some parts of the said river, to straighten the same by cutting away the banks, or by canal." In addition, they were given the power to enforce a clause of the incorporating act that required mill owners to erect locks where they had dammed the channel for water power.

The trustees chose four among their number to superintend the work at various points on the river. Richard N. Venable (1763–1838), a Prince Edward County lawyer, planter, and legislator, led this subgroup, which also included surveyor John Epperson. In anticipation of the various tasks laid out for them by the enabling legislation, Venable commissioned Epperson to survey the Appomattox. This resulting map illustrates the river's course from the site of Roger Atkinson's mill just west of Petersburg to the area around Cutbanks, about fifteen miles beyond Farmville. Epperson locates the sites of existing mills, bridges, fords, and falls; identifies the plantations of a number of prominent landholders along the waterway; and notes all the creeks and streams that feed the river on its way toward Petersburg.

ELS

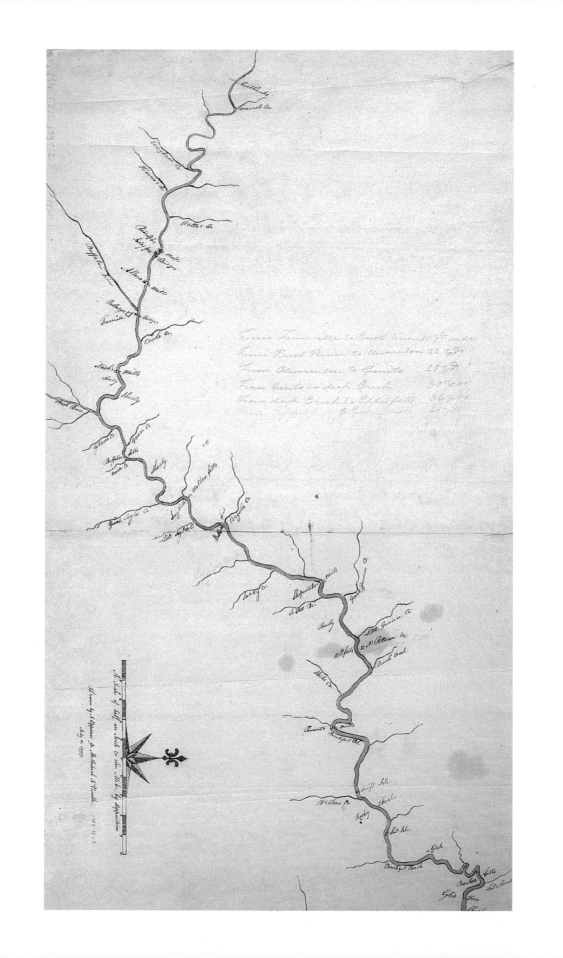

61   William Forsyth (1737–1804)

A Treatise on the Culture and Management of Fruit Trees; In Which A New Method Of Pruning and Training Is Fully Described
Philadelphia: Printed for J. Morgan, 1802
259 pp.

William Forsyth was a Scottish gardener from Aberdeenshire who was first employed at the Chelsea Physic Garden. In 1774 he built one of the first English rock gardens there, using old stone from the Tower of London and lava shipped in from Iceland. He later became the superintendent of the Royal Gardens at Kensington Palace. Soon after moving to London, he began to study tree growth and developed a plaster, which he claimed would cause new growth on diseased wood.

Although Forsyth's plaster remedy later proved worthless, his books became popular, and his *Treatise on the Culture and Management of Fruit Trees* went through numerous editions. This 1802 adaptation, with an introduction by William Cobbett, was the first book devoted to fruit alone to be published in America. The American editions of the book also retained the recipe for the miracle mixture Forsyth had prepared to treat diseased trees, as shown here in the plate of a stunted oak tree treated with the compound. John Graham, the owner of this copy, made extensive notes throughout the book and used it as a garden journal in which to record such entries as "Peach stone planted in Goochland 20 October 1813."

The brilliant yellow forsythia shrub that blooms in early spring was named in honor of Forsyth.

FSP

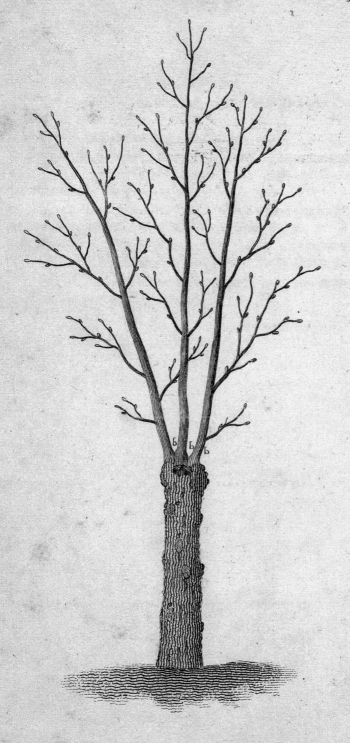

62 John Alexander Binns (ca. 1761–1831)

A Treatise on Practical Farming; Embracing Particularly the Following Subjects, viz. the Use of Plaister of Paris, with Directions for Using it: and General Observations on the Use of Other Manures
Frederick-town, Maryland: Printed by John B. Colvin, 1803
72 pp.

Virginians, such as John Alexander Binns, played an important role in the agricultural reforms of the early nineteenth century. Binns advocated deep plowing, raising clover to restore depleted soil, and the use of gypsum. He kept detailed records of his experiments with gypsum (known popularly then as plaster of paris) and significantly increased the yield of crops on his farm in Loudoun County.

Binns published his findings in 1803 in *A Treatise on Practical Farming*. The booklet sold for fifty cents and helped popularize the farming practices that became known as the "Loudoun system." His experiments caught the attention of Thomas Jefferson, who sent the treatise to several of his scientific friends here and abroad. Jefferson noted that Binns was a "plain farmer, who understands handling his plough better than his pen . . . the result of his husbandry proves his confidence in it well found for from being poor, it has made him rich." Some detractors criticized Binns for his extravagant claims about gypsum and felt that excessive use of it led to "sick" soil. Still others claimed that credit for the "Loudoun system" belonged to another Loudoun County resident, Israel Janney. Either way, the use of plaster and clover helped replenish soil exhausted by excessive tobacco growing.

FSP

A TREATISE

ON

PRACTICAL FARMING;

EMBRACING PARTICULARLY

THE FOLLOWING SUBJECTS, VIZ.

The Use of PLAISTER of PARIS, with Directions for Using it; and GENERAL OBSERVATIONS on the USE of OTHER MANURES.

On DEEP PLOUGHING; THICK SOWING of GRAIN; METHOD of PREVENTING FRUIT TREES from DECAYING, and

Farming in General.

By JOHN A. BINNS,
OF LOUDON COUNTY, VIRGINIA, FARMER.

FREDERICK-TOWN, MARYLAND,

Printed by JOHN B. COLVIN—Editor of the REPUBLICAN ADVOCATE.

1803.

63 Virginia Buggy Company Incorporated

[Catalog of] Virginia Buggy Company (Incorporated)
Builders of High-Grade Vehicles
Franklin, Virginia: n.p., n.d.
32 pp.

By the time John D. Abbitt opened his Virginia Buggy Company in 1910 in Franklin, Virginia, the first automobiles were already tooling around Southampton County. Abbitt may have guessed that the twentieth century was going to be the age of the wheel, but he anticipated that it would be pulled by horses, not horsepower. Franklin already supported several other coach companies, but that did not deter Abbitt. His catalog featured illustrations of buckboards, runabouts, buggies, and surreys. Customers could order special features, such as axles or a fifth wheel for spring buggies. The last page also offered suggestions for the care of these vehicles. Customers were cautioned to wash the carriages with clear, cold water and never to turn the hose on with force. Vehicles should be varnished at least once a year, and they should never be driven if the wheels were loose.

FSP

Virginia

BUGGY COMPANY

FRANKLIN,
VIRGINIA.

VI. *Body, Mind, and Soul*

64   **John Tennent (ca. 1700–ca. 1760)**

An Epistle to Dr. Richard Mead, Concerning the Epidemical Diseases of Virginia, Particularly A Pleurisy and Peripneumony . . .
Edinburgh: Printed by P. Matthie and sold by William Miller Bookseller, at his Shop a little above the Cross, North side of the Street, 1742
102 pp.

John Tennent arrived in Virginia from England about 1725 and settled in Spotsylvania County. What, if any, medical training he had is unknown. Nevertheless, by 1734 he had produced his first physiological treatise, *Every Man his own Doctor: or, The Poor Planter's Physician*. Printed by William Parks at Williamsburg, it enjoyed such popularity that it was reprinted twice in Philadelphia by Benjamin Franklin. It was his next treatise, *An Essay on Pleurisy*, published in 1736, that announced Tennent's life-long crusade, the therapeutic use of Virginia's native rattlesnake root for a wide variety of ailments. Introduced to him by the Seneca Indians, the herb was declared by Tennent to be particularly efficacious in the treatment of pleurisy and peripneumonia (pneumonia). "My success was so great," he claimed, "that I did not lose above four or five Patients in an Hundred, tho' other Practitioners lost two Thirds."

The next year he returned to London, where he made himself known to some of the city's leading lights of medicine. One of the most brilliant of these was Dr. Richard Mead, physician to the king and an intimate of such other notables as Isaac Newton, Alexander Pope, and Robert Walpole. Returning to Virginia in a typically choleric humor, Tennent was further disgruntled by the controversy his unorthodox cures had generated in the *Virginia Gazette*. Always willing to stir the pot, in 1738 he published an open letter to Dr. Mead (present here in the 1742 edition) in which he elaborated upon his extraordinary theories of disease and elevated rattlesnake root almost to a general panacea. Citing the "ingratitude of the colony," Tennent returned to England in 1739, where he spent the remainder of his life vainly striving for the recognition he felt was owed him.

RFS

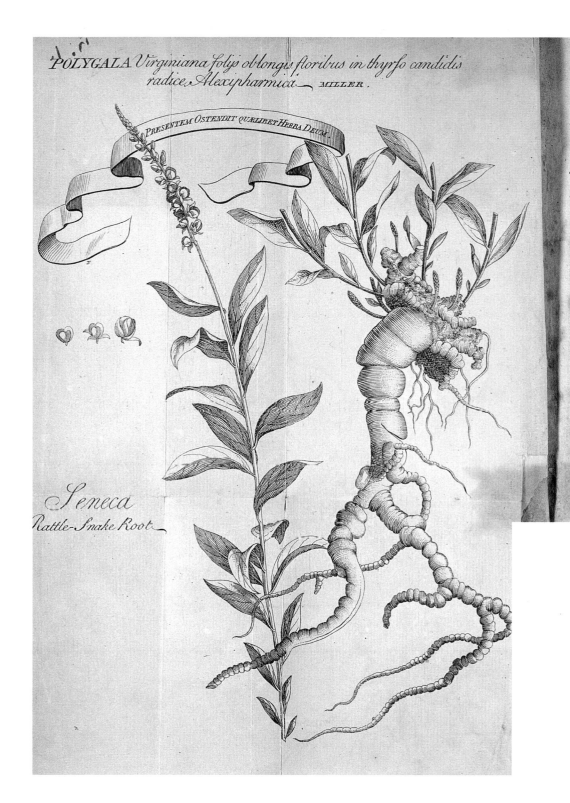

POLYGALA Virginiana folijs oblongis floribus in thyrso candidis radice Alexipharmica MILLER.

PRESENTEM OSTENDIT QUÆLIBET HERBA DEUM.

Seneca
Rattle-Snake Root

AN
EPISTLE
TO
Dr. RICHARD MEAD,
CONCERNING THE
Epidemical Diseases of VIRGINIA
PARTICULARLY,
A Pleurisy and Peripneumony:

Wherein is shewn the surprising Efficacy of the *Seneca Rattle-Snake Root*, in Diseases owing to a Viscidity and Co-agulation of the Blood; such as *Pleurisies* and *Peripneumonies*, these being epidemick, and very mortal in *Virginia*, and other Colonies on the Continent of *America*, and also the *Lee-Ward* Islands.

To which is prefixt,
A CUT of that most valuable PLANT:
And an APPENDIX annexed;

Demonstrating the highest Probability, that this Root will be of more extensive Use than any Medicine in the whole *Materia Medica*, and of curing the *Gout*, *Rheumatism*, *Dropsy*, and many nervous Diseases.

By JOHN TENNENT.

Natura, fortuna, providentia, fatum, nomina sunt unius Et ejusdem Dei, varie agentis in rebus humanis. SENECA.

EDINBURGH:
Printed by P. MATTHIE, and sold by WILLIAM MIL-LER Bookseller, at his Shop a little above the Cross, North Side of the Street. M.DCC.XLII.

65 John Brinsley (fl. 1633)

A Consolation for Our Grammar Schooles: or, A faithfull and most comfortable incouragement, for laying of a sure foundation of all good Learning in our Schooles, and for prosperous building thereupon . . .
London: Printed by Richard Field for Thomas Man dwelling in Pater noster Row, at the Signe of the Talbot, 1622
84 pp.

In this tract Brinsley enumerated the two principal duties of each of those who were charged with administering the remote and backward corners of Britain's fledgling empire. The first was to establish "pure religion, honor, and true worship" among his indigenous subjects, and the second was to "procure . . . the saving of all his poore people in those places, both of their soules and bodies." To achieve this, continued Brinsley, God had ordained "schooles of learning to be the principal meanes to reduce a barbarous people to civilitie. Marvel not," he cautioned, "if honest and upstanding Christians be so hardly drawn over to those places, as namely into Virginia, or so much as to perswade their friends to such a voyage, when as there are in the same so manifold perils, and especially of falling away from God to Sathan, and that themselves, or their posterity should become utterly savage as [the native inhabitants] are."

In fact, by the time Brinsley offered this exhortation, the Virginia Company already had set aside lands for the support of two such institutions, a college to acculturate the Indians and a university for the settlers, both at the town of Henricus. These were casualties of the uprising of 1622, the same year in which Brinsley's plea was printed, and no similar institutions of learning were attempted in Virginia until the College of William and Mary was established more than seventy years later.

RFS

A
CONSOLATION
FOR OVR GRAMMAR
SCHOOLES:
OR,

A faithfull and moſt comfortable incouragement, *for laying of a ſure foundation*
of all good Learning in our Schooles, and
for proſperous building thereupon.

More ſpecially for all thoſe of the inferiour
sort, and all ruder countries and places ; namely,
for *Ireland, Wales, Virginia,* with the *Sommer*
Ilands, and for their more ſpeedie attaining of our
Engliſh tongue by the ſame labour, that all
may ſpeake one and the ſame
Language.

And withall, for the helping of all ſuch as are de-
ſirous *ſpeedilie to recouer that which they had formerlie*
got in the Grammar Schooles; and to proceed aright
therein, for the perpetuall benefit of theſe our
Nations, and of the Churches
of Chriſt.

LONDON,
Printed by RICHARD FIELD for THOMAS MAN,
dwelling in Pater noſter Row, at the Signe
of the Talbot. 1622.

66 William Byrd II (1674–1744)

Letter, August 5, 1701, to Sir Robert Southwell
Manuscript
2 pp. 7 x 4½ in.

Virginia-born but reared and educated in England, William Byrd II made the acquaintance of British diplomat Sir Robert Southwell (1635–1702) sometime after completing his studies at the Middle Temple in London in 1695. Southwell took a liking to the young Virginian, securing him election as a fellow of the Royal Society, one of only two colonials ever to achieve that honor. Byrd, in turn, evinced the greatest respect for his elder. Years later he recalled that Southwell's "care and directions" influenced him greatly, while his introduction of Byrd "to the acquaintance of many of the first persons of his age" facilitated Byrd's own desires to mingle at the highest levels of British society. He would honor his mentor three decades after his death by hanging Southwell's portrait among those of a series of English notables in the elegant halls of his Westover mansion in Charles City County.

In 1701, Southwell persuaded Byrd to accompany his nephew, Sir John Perceval (1683–1748), on his grand tour of England. The younger man had left Oxford University without taking a degree, and perhaps Southwell thought Byrd might exert a proper influence on his ward while they progressed through the English countryside. In this letter, one of a series he wrote to Southwell in the summer of 1701, Byrd describes their visit to Cambridge University: "We din'd yesterday at Mr. Vice-Chancellour's, where Philosophy flew about the Table faster than the wine." With a parental-like pride, he also reported that "S[i]r John begins to make good discoverys of himself in company."

ELS

Cambridge y 5ᵗʰ August 1701.   3

Sr

Since our arrival at Cambridge I have had
the honour of one letter from you, and Sʳ John has received two. We have
been ever since wednesday surveying the university, and we owe a great
deal to our knowledge of this place to the information and Convoy of Mr
Colebatch. He is a man of distinction for learning and knowledge of
the world, and we had the happiness of having abundance of his company.
He desird me to let you know, that he is under great concern, that he
cant dispatch y affair you were pleas'd to commit to him, with so much
expedition as he promis'd. We dined yesterday at Mr Vice-chancellour's,
where Philosophy flew about the Table faster than the wine. Sr John
begins to make good discoverys of himself in company. We took a journy
on Saturday last to Audley Inn, about 12 miles from hence, which has y
name of being the largest house in Engᵈ. In our way we call'd at a house
of Mr Winstanlys, that built the light-house call'd Eddy-Stone off
Plymouth. Here are several of his contrivances, wᶜʰ like the greatest
part of modern philosophy, relish more of whimsy than advantage
to mankind. Amongst other things there's a Perpetual motion, performd
by a brass ball, that runs by a gentle declension down several spiral
ledges, til comeing to the bottom tis instantly drawn up ~~again~~ by a
Pully, and so repeats its tour again. From hence we proceeded to Saffron
Walden, where we met with a man very expert at planting & cureing y
commodity. You will not doubt but we took notes of so usefull a Process, and

Sr Robᵗ Southwell.

67 Thomas Jefferson (1743–1826)

Letter, October 14, 1785, Paris, France, to Samuel Henley
Manuscript
2 pp. 9 x 7¾ in.

Building his personal library was a task to which Thomas Jefferson enthusiastically devoted himself throughout his life. Among the many volumes he acquired were some sixty books obtained in 1778 from the library of the Reverend Samuel Henley, controversial former professor of moral philosophy at the College of William and Mary in Williamsburg. Henley had left the college hurriedly in 1775 to return to England, consigning his books to a fellow professor. Given the unsettled times, Jefferson never actually paid for his purchase. So, in 1785, while in Paris as American minister to France, Jefferson sought to close his account.

Not allowing the intervening time, or their political differences, to "dissolve the bands of private friendship," Jefferson likewise took pleasure in informing Henley of the current status of the college. While governor of Virginia, he had been instrumental in reforming the school, "having suppressed the two divinity schools & the grammar school, & substituted in their places a professorship of law (Mr. Wythe), another of Medicine, anatomy, chemistry & surgery (McClurg) and a third of Modern Languages (Bellini)." The move of Virginia's capital to Richmond in 1780 "made of Williamsburgh a mere academical village," but Jefferson still thought the "alteration" in the curriculum "has proved very succesful. They have now ordinarily about 80. students." The change of the seat of government ultimately proved more problematic than Jefferson imagined, however, and the college administration would struggle for a good fifty years before again securing the school on a firm financial and academic footing.

ELS

now remaining to me. I should be glad to hear that mr Gwat-
-kin has also succeeded to his mind.

You have been so long from Virginia, ~~the~~ that an account of
recent events would be scarcely intelligible to you without a knowlege of
what has preceded them. you know, doubtless of the removal of the seat
of government to Richmond. this has made of Williamsburgh a mere
academical village, disfigured by the burning of the president's house,
the palace & some others of smaller note. we have new modelled the
institution of the college, having suppressed the two divinity schools
& the grammar school & substituted in their places a professorship
of law (mr Wythe) another of Medecine, anatomy, chemistry & surge-
-ry (Mr Lwg) and a third of Modern languages. (Bellini) we were con-
-fined by the charter to six professorships & the legislature had
not leisure at that time to change the constitution of the college fun-
-damentally. the alteration has proved very successful. they have
now ordinarily about 80. students.   I shall hope the
pleasure of hearing from you, & am with great esteem
Dr. Sir

                    Your most obedient humble servt

                                        Th: Jefferson

68 John Donne (1573–1631)

A Sermon upon the VIII Verse of the I Chapter of the Acts of the Apostles. Preach'd To the Honourable Company of the Virginian Plantation. 13. Novemb. 1622
London: Printed by A. Mat: for Thomas Jones and are to be sold at his Shop in the Strand, at the blacke Rauen, neere unto Saint Clements Church, 1622
49 pp.

Recognized as one of the most eloquent and able speakers of his day, preacher-poet John Donne was admitted to membership in the London Company at a troubled time in the colony's existence. The company was not succeeding as well as its shareholders had hoped, and there was continuing friction between those who viewed the enterprise in purely commercial terms and a minority, including Sir Edward Sandys, Nicholas Ferrar, and Lord Southampton, an early friend and patron of William Shakespeare, who were animated by loftier religious goals. Donne's sermon sounded a chord in sympathy with this latter group and has been described as the first missionary sermon printed in the English language. "As God taught us to make cloathes, not onely to cloath our selves, but to cloath his poore and naked members heere; as God taught us to build houses, not to house our selves, but to house him in erecting Churches, to his glory: So God taught us to make Ships, not to transport our selves, but to transport him. . . ." The original edition sold out quickly, as did every one of Donne's sermons printed during his lifetime. Original imprints of these discourses are now quite rare.

RFS

A
SERMON
VPON
THE VIII. VERSE
OF THE I. CHAP-
TER OF THE ACTS
OF THE APOSTLES.

Preach'd

To the Honourable Company of the
VIRGINIAN PLANTATION.
13º. *Nouemb.* 1622.

BY
IOHN DONNE *Deane of* St.
Pauls, London.

LONDON.
Printed by A. MAT: for THOMAS IONES
and are to fold at his Shop in the Strand, at the
blacke *Rauen,* neere vnto Saint
Clements Church.
1622.

69   William Castell (d. 1645)

A Petition of W. C. Exhibited to the High Court of Parliament now assembled, for the propagating of the Gospel in America, and the West Indies; and for the settling of our Plantations there, which Petition is approved by 70 able English Divines. Also by Master Alexander Henderson, and some other worthy Ministers of Scotland

[London]: n.p., 1641

19 pp.

Castell was among the first after the uprising of 1622 to suggest that Parliament should recognize the benefits to be accrued by the English colonies by cultivating the friendship of the Indians and converting them to Protestant Christianity. By these means he hoped not only to promote tranquillity, but also to protect both the Indians and the English from the anticipated rapacity of the Spaniards, who still claimed rights over the whole of America. Noting earlier, half-hearted efforts to convert "those silly seduced *Americans*" to Christianity, Castell chided those of "the reformed religion" for having either "placed themselves in the skirts of *America*, where there are but few natives (as those of new *England*), or else for want of able and conscionable Ministers (as in *Virginia*) they themselves are become exceedingly rude, more likely to turne Heathen, [than] to turne others to the Christian faith."

There is no doubt that this petition created widespread interest in the welfare of the colony, so much so that shortly after its appearance, an ordinance was passed by Parliament appointing Robert, earl of Warwick, "Governor Chief of all the Plantations in America," with a committee to "be assisting unto him, for the better governing, strengthening, and preservation of the said Plantations; but chiefly for the advancement of the . . . Gospel of Christ among those that yet remain there in great and miserable blindnesse and ignorance."

RFS

A
PETITION
OF *W.C.*
EXHIBITED
TO THE HIGH
COVRT OF Parliament

now assembled, for the propagating of the Gospel in
America, and the *West Indies*; and
for the setling of our Plantations
there; which Petition is approved by 70 *able English*
Divines.

Also by Master *Alexander Henderson,*
and some other worthy Ministers
of Scotland.

Printed in the yeare, 1641.

70 Thomas Bray (1658–1730)

A Memorial, Representing the Present State of Religion, on the Continent of North America
London: Printed by William Downing, for the Author, 1700
15 pp.

As Bray biographer John Wolfe Lydekker observed, if anyone deserved to be ranked among the "post-reformation" saints, it was Anglican divine Thomas Bray, "for no man did more for the Church at home and abroad, and no man received less from her in the way of earthly compensation." A native of Shropshire, the young clergyman's erudite yet popular writings brought him to the attention of the bishop of London, who, in 1695, appointed him as the first commissary over the Anglican churches in Maryland. He immediately became active in sending missionaries and in founding parochial libraries in Maryland, Virginia, and other British colonies so that locally recruited clergy could properly be trained. Altogether he established no fewer than thirty-nine libraries, some of which contained more than a thousand volumes.

When Bray returned to England after visiting Maryland in 1700, he found that the Quakers, who enjoyed an unusual degree of religious freedom in that colony, "had raised prejudice" against the establishment of the Anglican church in Maryland. He contested their arguments in this *Memorial,* which also lavished praise upon Virginia's governor, Francis Nicholson, and soon a bill was passed for the maintenance of the established church. This report had much to do with the founding in 1701 of the Society for the Propagation of the Gospel in Foreign Parts, which remained extremely influential in Virginia and throughout the other American colonies, and continues its world missionary work to this day.

RFS

A

MEMORIAL,

REPRESENTING THE

PRESENT STATE

OF

RELIGION,

ON THE

CONTINENT

OF

North-America.

By THOMAS BRAY, D. D.

LONDON,

Printed by *William Downing*, for the Author, 1700.

71   Francis Makemie (1658–1708)

A Plain and Friendly Perswasive to the Inhabitants of Virginia and Maryland, For Promoting Towns and Cohabitation. By a Well-Wisher to both Governments

London: Printed by John Humfreys, in Bartholomew-lane, 1705

16 pp.

Generally regarded as the founder of the Presbyterian Church in America, Makemie was born in County Donegal, Ireland. He graduated from Glasgow University and, shortly thereafter, was ordained and sent to America as a missionary. By 1683 he had arrived on Maryland's Eastern Shore, where he established the first regular Presbyterian church in North America and began to travel widely as an evangelist. A combination of marriage and a generous bequest settled him on Virginia's Eastern Shore. His father-in-law was a wealthy Accomack County tradesman whose death in 1698 left Makemie with sufficient means to establish himself as a merchant and land trader. His pursuit of worldly endeavors did not, however, diminish his Calvinistic fervor, and soon after he was arrested for preaching without a license and was sent to Williamsburg for trial. So successfully did he argue his case in 1699 that he was granted a license to preach. He thus became the first dissenting minister licensed under England's Toleration Act of 1689 in a colony not noted for its religious tolerance.

In the years 1704–1705 he traveled to England, where he published *A Plain and Friendly Perswasive*. Reflecting the author's own professional dichotomy of the spiritual and the secular, Makemie's dissertation urged the construction of "ports, towns and cohabitation" on one hand, and the encouragement of "education and vertue" on the other. Like those who had commented upon conditions in the colony during the preceding century, Makemie felt that if future settlement could be concentrated into communities, both the moral and material well-being of the population would be improved.

By 1707 he was again defending the rights of nonconformists, this time in New York, where his vigorous defense of religious freedom ultimately led to the recall of his antagonist, Gov. Thomas Cornbury. Returning to Virginia, he died shortly thereafter.

RFS

A

Plain and Friendly

PERSWASIVE

TO THE

INHABITANTS

OF

VIRGINIA

AND

MARYLAND,

For Promoting

Towns and Cohabitation.

By a Well-Wisher to both Governments.

LONDON,
Printed by *John Humfreys,* in *Bartholomew-lane,* 1705.

VII. *The World of African Americans*

72   Author unknown

The Case of Separate Traders to Africa with Remarks on the African Company's Memorial
London: n.p., 1709
4 pp.

      By 1760, the number of imported Africans had increased to 188,600. This document illuminates the involvement of Africans in the trade. Traders reported that "On the Gold Coast the natives come up and down the coast." Trading above and below the forts, they arrived "in boats bringing gold, Negroes, and elephant teeth, which they sell to the ships out at sea." In the event that "no English ships are there, they sell them to the Portuguese ships, or Dutch interlopers." The greatest market for slaves was at Widah, "situated about 40 or 50 leagues below the Gold Coast." Denouncing a monopoly on the slave trade, the separate traders claimed "nothing hath given so great encouragement to the trade of Britain, as our Gentry bringing up their children to foreign trade." Appealing to those members of society who already had a stake in the slave trade, the separate traders asked, "must our gentry send their younger sons abroad, to be bred up in foreign affairs? Or must they send them into other countries to learn trade and settle?" This document, as well as the one regarding *The Falsities of Private Traders to Africa*, amplifies the highly competitive and commercial nature of the Atlantic slave trade and hence its perpetuation.

LLL

The CASE of the *Separate Traders* to *Africa*.

BEtween the Years 1672, and 1698. the present *African* Company enjoyed the Trade to *Guinea* by Patent from King *Charles*, exclusive of all others; but on the repeated Complaints from the Plantations, of their not being supplied by the said Company with a sufficient Number of Negroes, the Trade was laid open by Act of Parliament in 1698, to all the Subjects of *England* to trade to alike, on paying 10 *per Cent.* on Exports, for supporting Forts, *&c.* who improved it to such a Height in a Year or two, that there were employed 5 times the Number of Ships, and the Plantations were supplied with 5 times the Number of Negroes as by the Company, when exclusive, as appears by an Account lately sent from *Barbados*, of the Numbers delivered into that Island in 10 Years past, being 7000 and odd by the Company, and 27000 and odd by Separate Traders, and in proportion to all the other Plantations, supplying the Spaniards with great Numbers besides.

Virginia and *Maryland* sufficiently discover the vast Benefit of the Increase of this Trade by Separate Traders. The former having been supplied but with very few Negroes in many Years by the Company, when exclusive; the latter (where almost all the Tobacco fit for Foreign Markets is produced) with none at all, and the Possessors of many thousand Acres of uncultivated Ground forced to work alone on their own Land bare-foot and bare-legg'd. But since the Act for laying open the Trade to *Africa*, that Province hath been so abundantly supplied with Negroes by Separate Traders, that it now makes yearly 30000 Hogsheads of Tobacco fit for the Consumption of our Neighbours: To the great Increase of Navigation at home, and our vast Benefit in the Ballance of Trade abroad.

The Money arising by the Ten *per Cent.* Duty since the said Act, hath amounted to near 90000 *l.* as the Accounts kept thereof make appear, which is more by near one half than is necessary for Support of all the Forts and Settlements in *Guinea* under any tolerable Rules of good Husbandry, tho' three times the Number of Soldiers, Ammunition, *&c.* had been provided, as ever were by the Company, who nevertheless have kept them in so sorry a Condition, that the best of their Forts have surrendred to the first Demands that were ever made of them this War by the French; and the Separate Traders, instead of Protection, daily receive very ill Treatment from the Company's Agents and Factors, who by secret Practices and open Violence, have often ruined their Voyages, so much to the Discouragement of the said Separate Traders, that they dare not come near the English Settlements ashore; *but are forced to trade with the Natives out at Sea, by which means they have never proved of any Advantage to Separate Traders, nor answered the End intended by keeping them.*

The Exports for *Africa* loaded with the 10 *per Cent.* Duty, consisting 5 Parts in 6 of the Woollen and other Manufactures of *Great Britain*, the Separate Traders are on a very unequal foot with those of other Nations, by means of that Duty, who can sell all Commodities proper for that Country Ten *per Cent.* cheaper than the Subjects of *Great Britain*: Whereas were the Money raised by the said Duty rightly applied, two Thirds, or one Half thereof, would be sufficient to maintain the said Forts.

The Act of Parliament obliges the Company's Stock as a Security for the well maintaining the Forts, and justly laying out the Money arising from the Ten *per Cent.* Duty, whereby being prevented making Dividends, they found out an Expedient to evade the Intention of the Act, by giving Bottomree-Bonds to their Members to pay 125 *l.* on Arrival of the first of their Ships, for 100 *l.* borrowed; by which means they have divided out their Stock and Ten *per Cent.* Money also, *slighting the Trade*; and thereby they are become worse than Nothing, by a very great Sum; Nevertheless produce fictitious Accompts of their Charges on Forts (wherein their chief Factor, Accomptant, Warehouse-keeper, and Gold-taker, are stiled Generals and Lieutenant Generals, to about 30 or 40 Soldiers, with near 4000 *l. per Annum* Salaries) clamouring they are undone by supporting the said Forts, tho 'twill appear they are indebted to the Ten *per Cent.* Duty a great Sum.

Several of the Forts pretended to by the Company were built out of the Ten *per Cent.* Duty, and *Cabo Corso*, worth all the rest, is undoubtedly the Nation's Property, being taken from the Dutch at the Nation's Charge; for tho King *Charles* granted this Company a Patent for the sole Trade, exclusive of all others, together with that Place, that Patent was disregarded by the Parliament in 1698. and all the Settlements in *Guinea* render'd free for all English Men to live in; and this Company trusted but for 13 Years with the said Settlements, and the Trade laid open to all.

The Company argue, that Negroes are become dear on the Coast, by reason of many Buyers, which is rather occasioned by their Factors selling them to the *Portuguese*, as well as by a greater Number than formerly carry'd to the Plantations, which are there sold so low, that the Planters have Negroes now for 1 ½ and 2 Hogsheads of Sugar *per Head*, which they used to give the Company seven Hogsheads for, when the Trade was exclusive.

The most clamorous Enemies against the Separate Traders, are the Purchasers of the Company's Bonds, who make all the Interest they can in assisting the Company to get an exclusive Act; by which Means they expect the Bonds they bought at 50 *per Cent.* Discount, will come to be paid, if the Separate Traders can be destroyed. Which is the same thing as if the Creditors of any other Bankrupt should make an Interest, that all those of that Bankrupt Trade or Profession should be turn'd out of their Business, and the other put in; that thereby he might be enabled to pay them their full Debts: And the Mine-Adventure Company have the same Reason to petition the Parliament, that all the Lead-Mines in *England* may be stopt up, and none work'd in but such as belong to that Company, that they might be thereby enabled to pay their Debts also.

To erect an *African* Company exclusive, is to subject the Trade of one half of the World, the Trade of *Africa* and *America*, and the Navigation depending thereon, to but one Person; which would prove a Monopoly, in every respect, the most grievous to the Subject of any in the worst of times, being effectually three Companies under one Denomination, a Woollen Manufacture Company at home, a Negroe Company in the Plantations; and in short, a general *West-India Company*, who would have the Power of laying what Excise they pleased on the Productions of our Plantations, consumed at home and abroad; and Confinement of Trades to such Mo-

nopolies

73 Author unknown

The Falsities of private traders to Africa discover'd and the mischiefs they occasion demonstrated and an account of the settlements on that coast purchased, built, and now possest, by the Company

London: n.p., 1709

4 pp.

The African Company claimed that "the private traders to Africa have been, and are a very great burthen upon the company, a molestation to the government on the coast, a prejudice to that of the trade of the nation, and to the plantations and colonies; and that without some immediate relief, the whole is in danger of being totally lost."

In the eighteenth century, when England took a leading role in the slave trade, it established and maintained trading posts in Africa at Gambia and along the lower Guinea coast. The Cape Coast Castle became the center of slave trade in Africa. Most of the enslaved Africans came from the Senegal River to southern Angola. Nearly one-fourth came from Angola, and a smaller number were brought in from the Bight of Biafra.

Slaves represented a major category of taxable property. The import duty was the earliest form of taxation, although the methods by which slaves were taxed varied widely and oftentimes were controversial. As the number of slave importations increased, legislators recognized the duty as a source of revenue and thereafter increased it.

Scholars Robert Fogel and Stanley Engerman estimate that between 1620 and 1700 nearly 20,500 Africans were brought into British North America and the area we now know as Louisiana. This document estimates that 25,000 Africans were needed annually to supply the English plantations and colonies. The majority went to Jamaica and the Spanish West Indies (12,000); Virginia, Barbados, and the Leeward Islands each received 4,000, while Carolina and New York received 1,000 enslaved Africans.

LLL

Some OBSERVATIONS on EXTRACTS taken out of the Report from the Lords Commissioners for *Trade* and *Plantations*.

1st Extract. THE Number of *Negroes* yearly Imported into the *English* Plantations and Colonies, since the time of Passing the Act of Parliament by the private Traders, being (as they compute) about 25000.

2. That generally the Prices in the Plantations have been from 14 to *l.* 23 *per* Head.

3. 'Tis computed that the Number of *Negroes*, necessary for a yearly Supply of the Plantations, is

For *Virginia* and *Maryland*	4000
Carolina and *New-York*	1000
Barbadoes	4000
Leeward-Islands	4000
For the Use of *Jamaica*, and what are carried by Her Majesty's Subjects to the *Spanish West-Indies*,	12000
	25000

Which Number of 25000, the private Traders reckon have been Imported to those several Colonies.

4. 'Tis alledged by the Company, that the Natives on the Coast enjoy the whole Benefit of the Trade, taking advantage of different Traders to advance the Prices of *Negroes*, and their own Goods, and to depreciate our Merchandizes; and they add in discourse, that the Price of *Negroes* is now about Ten Pounds *per* Head in *Africa*, whereas formerly it was not above Three.

This the private Traders admit to be true in the manner as is before mention'd.

5. The Company say, they understand the best Establishment to be a Joint Stock, exclusive of all others : But in case that shall not be thought proper, they say they will be content to be limited in their Trade from *Cape-Blanco* to *Cape-Lopez*, if the private Traders be restrain'd from coming there.

To this the private Traders answer, That whatever Confusion may have happened in that Trade, they are to be imputed to the different Interests of the Company and private Traders. Therefore, for prevention of the like for the future, they propose that all Traders to *Africa* be set on an equal Foot, by laying open the Trade, like that to *Turkey*.

To set this in a more true Light, in order to give a right Judgment thereof, 'tis necessary to premise the following Particulars.

1st. Partic. To know the Annual Exports of the private Traders, which are, as appears by their own Oaths and Entries in the Custom-house of *London, Bristol*, and other Out-Ports of *England* successively, for Six Years last past, *viz.*

	l.	*s.*	*d.*
From 29th *September* 1701, to 29th *September* 1702	37875	18	6
29th *September* 1702, to 29th *September* 1703	44115	12	3
29th *September* 1703, to 29th *September* 1704	26527	07	11
29th *September* 1704, to 29th *September* 1705	30651	07	6
29th *September* 1705, to 29th *September* 1706	32144	19	6
29th *September* 1706, to 29th *September* 1707	31986	16	8

The whole Six Years amounts to ———— *l.* 203302 : 02 : 4

Which in an Averidge is 33883 *l.* 13 *s.* 8 *d. per Annum*, their whole Exports from *England*.

2d Partic. That Fortifications and Settlements on the Coast, and an equal Strength with other *European* Nations, are absolutely necessary to be maintain'd, for Preservation of the *British* Interest, with the Natives.

That for preserving and increasing Trade to the said Settlements, it is also as necessary, that by Policy and Presents, Friendship be kept up betwixt Natives and Natives, and as many of them as possible brought into, and continued in the Interest of the Settlements, without which the Trade to them will be intercepted; and upon occasion of any Quarrel, those Friends must be supported against the Friends of other *Europeans*; and that the only way to have no interruption in Trade, is, to preserve the Balance of Power.

This Occasions sometimes a very great and uncertain Expence of Goods, Ammunition and Arms ; and as the Settlements are numerous, and under divers Petty Kings, they are seldom free from Differences amongst one or more of their Neighbours, Friends to other *Europeans* ; Also they are illiterate People, and have not (or are they govern'd by) any Religion, Laws or Courts of Justice, or any civiliz'd Rules of Discipline.

The best Foundation and Establishment of the Native's Friendship, Justice, Humanity and Honesty is their dependance on the Protection, Assistance and Benefit from the Forts and Settlements, which ceases when the Trade is supplied by different Interests, and the whole falls into Confusion and Disorder.

That

74   Virginia House of Burgesses

Petition, 1772, to King George III of England
Manuscript
1 p. 13¾ x 26½ in.

When the Virginia House of Burgesses unanimously authorized this petition in April 1772, its plea to King George III capped a five-year effort to end, or at least constrict, the Atlantic slave trade. Drafted in all likelihood by Richard Henry Lee and signed by Peyton Randolph, the House speaker who would soon preside over the Continental Congress in Philadelphia, the address seemed to arise from the most altruistic of motives. "The Importation of Slaves into the Colonies from the Coast of Africa hath long been considered as a Trade of great Inhumanity, and . . . we have too much Reason to fear will endanger the very Existence of your Majesty's American Dominions," declared the burgesses. They claimed the trade "greatly retards the Settlement of the Colonies, with more useful Inhabitants, and may, in Time, have the most destructive Influence."

In reality, the burgesses harbored a number of ulterior economic motives, as summarized by Woody Holton in his recent book, *Forced Founders* (1999). They anticipated that hindering the foreign slave trade with high import duties might reduce the number of laborers in the colony, thus driving up the price of tobacco; trim the flow of cash out of the colony; eliminate competition to the domestic slave trade; encourage the immigration of artisans and craftsmen; and decrease the potential for slave insurrections. Not surprisingly, George III and his ministers rejected the proposal, leading Thomas Jefferson to include the monarch's "suppressing every legislative attempt to prohibit or to restrain this execrable commerce" as one of the charges against the king in his draft of the Declaration of Independence.

ELS

To the King's most Excellent Majesty.

The humble Address of the House of Burgesses
OF *Virginia*

Most Gracious Sovereign.

We your Majesty's dutiful and loyal Subjects the Burgesses of Virginia, now met in General Assembly, beg Leave with all Humility, to approach your Royal Presence.

The many Instances of your Majesty's benevolent Intentions and most gracious Disposition to promote the Prosperity, and Happiness of your Subjects in the Colonies encourage us to look up to the Throne, and implore your Majesty's paternal Assistance in averting a Calamity of a most alarming Nature.

The Importation of Slaves into the Colonies from the Coast of Africa hath long been considered as a Trade of great Inhumanity, and under its present Encouragement, we have too much reason to fear will endanger the very Existence of your Majesty's American Dominions.

We are sensible that some of your Majesty's Subjects in Great Britain may reap Emoluments from this sort of Traffick, but when we consider that it greatly retards the Settlement of the Colonies with more useful Inhabitants, and may, in Time, have the most destructive Influence, we presume to hope that the Interest of a few will be disregarded, when placed in Competition with the Security and Happiness of such Numbers of your Majesty's dutiful and loyal Subjects.

Deeply impressed with these Sentiments, we most humbly beseech your Majesty to remove all those Restraints on your Majesty's Governors of this Colony which inhibit their assenting to such Laws, as might check so very pernicious a Commerce. Your Majesty's ancient Colony and Dominion of Virginia hath at all Times and upon every Occasion been entirely devoted to your Majesty's sacred Person and Government, and we cannot forego this Opportunity of renewing those Assurances of the truest Loyalty, and warmest Affection, which we have so often, with the greatest Sincerity, given to the best of Kings, whose Wisdom and Goodness we esteem the surest Pledges of the Happiness of all his People.

Peyton Randolph Speaker

75 The Pennsylvania Society for the Promoting of the Abolition of Slavery and the Relief of Free Negroes Unlawfully held in bondage and for improving the condition of the African Race

Memorials presented to the Congress of the United States of America by the Different Societies, Instituted for Promoting the Abolition of Slavery, etc. in the States of Rhode-Island, Connecticut, New-York, Pennsylvania, Maryland, and Virginia

Philadelphia: Francis Bailey, 1792

31 pp.

Before the American Revolution, the religious group most vocal in advocating the emancipation of slaves was the Quakers. They believed that the inner light of God was within each person and therefore that each person was fundamentally equal. In 1775 Quaker abolitionist Anthony Benezet organized the first antislavery society in the world. By 1787 it had become the Pennsylvania Society for the Promoting of the Abolition of Slavery, and its first president was Benjamin Franklin. A society was founded in Delaware in 1788; one in Maryland followed in 1789. By the end of the eighteenth century, New Jersey, Connecticut, and Virginia had formed abolitionist societies, many of them headed by Quakers.

Several such societies are represented in this collection of petitions. The president of the Rhode Island society, David Howell, stated that the slaveholders "accumulated private wealth." Connecticut's Ezra Stiles, who was also president of Yale University as well as a prominent Congregational minister, advocated liberty and religious freedom. Matthew Clarkson, vice president of the New York society, declared that the slave trade was a "disgraceful traffic" and believed that it was imperative the country "lessen the miseries of the enslaved." Andrew Swearingen, vice president of the Washington, D.C., society, also urged the country to "lessen the miseries of the unhappy Negroes," specifically referring to "their passage by sea." Daniel McCurtin and Robert Pleasants, presidents of abolitionist groups in Maryland and Virginia, respectively, wrote similar impassioned pleas.

During the 1780s Quakers throughout the North strongly urged their members to emancipate their slaves. Many Congregational and Methodist clergy supported the Quakers. Slavery gradually dwindled in the North, but the South resisted change.

LLL

MEMORIALS

PRESENTED TO THE

CONGRESS

OF THE

United States of America,

BY THE

DIFFERENT SOCIETIES

INSTITUTED FOR PROMOTING THE

ABOLITION OF SLAVERY, &c. &c.

IN THE STATES OF

RHODE-ISLAND, CONNECTICUT, NEW-
YORK, PENNSYLVANIA, MARY-
LAND, AND VIRGINIA.

PUBLISHED BY ORDER OF "THE PENNSYLVANIA SOCIETY FOR PRO-
MOTING THE ABOLITION OF SLAVERY, AND THE RELIEF OF FREE
NEGROES UNLAWFULLY HELD IN BONDAGE, AND FOR IM-
PROVING THE CONDITION OF THE AFRICAN RACE."

PHILADELPHIA:
PRINTED BY Francis Bailey, No. 116, HIGH-STREET.

M DCC XCII.

76A   Nimrod Farrow (1765–1830)

Letter, March 16, 1829, to Doctor Robert McKey Stribling and Captain Stephen Chilton
Manuscript
4 pp. 9¾ x 8 in.

76B   Keeble, Hannah

Authorization, January 14, 1828, issued to John Ogilvie to baptize Ben, an African American slave
Manuscript
1 p. 5 x 8 in.

Upper Goose Creek Baptist Church was founded in 1799 at Farrowsville, near present-day Markham, in Fauquier County, Virginia. Like so many congregations of that day, the members of Goose Creek struggled to find a permanent location for their worship services, which in the first third of the nineteenth century included a substantial portion of African American members. To their great relief, in 1819 Nimrod Farrow and his wife, Dolly, deeded three acres on which was constructed a "house of Publick Worship." Farrow, famed locally for his role in the construction of Fort Gaines at the entrance to Mobile Bay, envisioned a union church that would be available to all denominations. The Baptists of Goose Creek, however, were to take precedence, having the first choice in meeting dates and times.

In his letter to two of the Goose Creek trustees, Farrow reviewed the history of his gift and provided a sketch of the site. Revealing the limited nature of African American church membership, he divided the grounds surrounding the meetinghouse into a yard for horses, a "Front yard . . . sufficient to accommodate from Eight Hundred to One Thousand white people with comfort & ease," and a "yard set a part for Coloured people, sufficient to accommodate from two to three hun[dre]d."

Hannah Keeble, whose slave Ben had "a noshan of joinin your Church," wrote in 1828 to John Ogilvie (1793–1849), pastor at Goose Creek, authorizing his baptism. "We have owned Ben Ever sense A small Boy," she reported, "and have found him to Be honest truthfull and [an] Obedient servant."

ELS

This is the line from the creek between Col[?] Full[?] & myself to the road &c

Spring

Road to the Spring

Front yard including the meeting House, sufficient to accommodate from Eight to one thousand white people with comfort & ease.

meetinghouse

Back yard at a distance below? Stay people, sufficient to accommodate from two to three hun?

Yard for Horses, sufficient for any number of Horses on common occasions and much to spare.

Road to the Creek

Dear sir

My Ben tels me that he has A. ~~feeling~~ Noshan of Joining your Church and if you thinks proper to Receve him J have No Objecktion to his Bein Baptise? We have owned Ben Ever sense A small Boy and have found him to Be honest truthfull and Obidient ~~your~~ servant

Hannah Keeble

January 14th 182.8

77 Baptist Brethren of Colour. Buck Marsh Corresponding Meeting.

Minutes of the Buck Marsh Corresponding Meeting of Baptist Brethren of Colour, held at Winchester
Meeting House, Frederick County, Va., Whitsunday and Monday, 1829
Winchester, Virginia: S. H. Davis, 1829
4 pp.

    This document illuminates the inner workings of an antebellum religious council. By 1814 a few Baptist
churches were composed entirely of African Americans, both free and enslaved. The majority of black Baptists,
however, were members of the same churches as their owners. Most black churches were included in district associations along with white churches.

    On June 7 and 8, 1829, the Winchester Meeting House hosted the fourth meeting of the Baptist Brethren
of Colour. Present were eight ministers and fifteen messengers from eleven churches: Buck Marsh, Winchester,
Salem, Bethel, Zoar, Waterlick, Zion, Opequon, Happy Creek, Back Lick, and Upperville. At this meeting the
Upperville church sought membership in the association and was admitted. All those in attendance contributed
fifty cents to the general fund. Members of the group were chosen as treasurer, and a committee of three was
appointed to count the contributions. The council resolved to purchase a book in which to keep minutes. Another committee was formed to arrange the preaching for the two-day meeting. Also during the meeting the
brethren discussed the withdrawal of the "coloured part of Salem church." The following day the council appointed the future speaker for the introductory sermon. In addition, a schedule of visits to various churches in
the association was made. Furthermore, one of the members was appointed to superintend the printing of the
minutes. The members also decided where to hold a subsequent meeting. Finally, they granted permission for
one of the churches to "unite with other churches in forming a new corresponding meeting."

LLL

FOURTH MEETING......1829.

MINUTES

OF THE

Buck Marsh Corresponding Meeting

OF

BAPTIST BRETHREN OF COLOUR,

HELD AT WINCHESTER MEETING-HOUSE,

Frederick county, Va.

WHITSUNDAY AND MONDAY....1829.

LORD'S DAY, JUNE 7, 1829.

The meeting met pursuant to adjournment.

1. The introductory sermon was preached by brother Thomas Whiting, from Romans viii. 10. "And if Christ be in you, the body is dead because of sin; but the spirit is life because of righteousness."

2. After a short intermission the following ministers and messengers appeared and took their seats:

Churches.	Ministers.	Messengers.	min.	fund
Buck marsh,	Thomas Whiting.	William Riley, Norbin Sample.	50	50
Winchester,	Jonathan Robinson.	Dean Johnson, William Dixon.	50	50
Salem,	None.	None.		
Bethel,	Thomas Whiting.	Harry Reed, Robert Cook.	50	50
Zoar,	Martin Robinson.	Martin Robinson.	50	50
Waterlick,	John Halbert.	Harry Blan, Harry Wells.	50	50
Zion,	James Pollard.	George Johnson.	50	50
Opequon,	None.	James Fairfax, Jerry Monroe.	50	50
Happy creek,	John Halbert.	John Halbert.	50	50
Back lick,	John Bossey.	John Bossey.	50	
Upperville,	Reuben Moss, Benjamin Moss.	John Moren.	50	50
			500	450

[The Upperville church applied to be received at this meeting, and was admitted by giving its messenger the right hand of fellowship.]

78   Lefevre James Cranstone (ca. 1820–1867)

"Negro Shanty, Virginia," 1860
Watercolor on paper. 11¾ x 6 in.

From September 1859 through June 1860, English artist Lefevre James Cranstone traveled through the eastern and midwestern United States, recording scenes of everyday life throughout Virginia and present-day West Virginia, Washington, D.C., Kentucky, Ohio, Indiana, and New York. During his American sojourn, Cranstone produced more than 360 watercolor sketches.

Here Cranstone records a scene (probably near Wheeling, Virginia, later part of West Virginia) that may have been intended as a refutation of a popular mid-nineteenth-century pro-slavery argument that African Americans were lesser beings unable to care properly for themselves. Every element in this watercolor suggests order and prosperity.

The small but substantial house in the foreground is tightly weatherboarded, well covered with a standing-seam metal roof, lit by light through generous amounts of (expensive) glass, and surrounded with a tightly planked, horizontally boarded fence. The standing African American woman is well dressed, her hair neatly arranged, and her bright blue dress is covered by a spotless white apron.

The house in the background, a Rhenish-American banked house, would have incorporated areas for both work and storage. Farm animals would have been housed there. The yard is fenced with a closely boarded fence, which was used to enclose poultry and small livestock such as pigs. Two purple martin boxes to the left of the house lean over a shelter for poultry. Martins were considered particularly beneficial birds on a farm because they voraciously eat insects. They also had a reputation for driving away the crows and hawks that preyed upon chickens. Because German-speaking farmers rarely owned slaves, the African American woman in the foreground probably was free.

BCG

79 Thomas P. Fenner (1829–1912)

Cabin and Plantation Songs as Sung by the Hampton Students
New York: G. P. Putnam's Sons, 1876
225 pp.

    In 1872 Gen. Samuel Armstrong, the founder of Hampton Institute, and Thomas Fenner, the musical director, created a choral group named the Hampton Singers. The group was modeled after Fisk University's successful Jubilee Choir. Like that choir, the Hampton Singers toured major cities to raise funds. On the tour, Armstrong solicited support from members of the northeastern elite. Both Armstrong and the Hampton Singers were so successful that they devoted the spring and summer portions of each year to a northern fund-raising campaign.

    Many of these songs originated in the realm of work. A favorite song among the hands in the tobacco factories in Danville, Virginia, was "Bright Sparkles in de Churchyard" (p. 200). Another song, "I Hope My Mother Will Be There" (p. 218), was also known as the Mayo Boys' Song and was sung by the hands in Mayo's tobacco factory in Richmond, Virginia. Several of the songs first published in this collection are "Judgment Day Is a-Rolling Round," "Keep Me from Sinkin' Down," and "I've Been a-List'ning All de Night Long." Mahalia Jackson (1911–1972), known as the Queen of Gospel Song, recorded several of the spirituals included in this collection. Most notable are "In Dat Great Gittin' Up Mornin'" and "Move On Up a Little Higher." Many of the spirituals included in this publication are still sung in black Baptist churches today. One of the most frequently sung is "Nobody Knows de Trouble I've Seen" (p. 181).

LLL

178

CABIN

AND

PLANTATION SONGS

AS SUNG BY THE

HAMPTON STUDENTS.

ARRANGED BY

THOMAS P. FENNER,

In Charge of Musical Department of the Hampton Normal and Agricultural Institute of Virginia.

NEW YORK:
G. P. PUTNAM'S SONS,
FOURTH AVE. & 23D STREET.
1876.

VIII. *The World of Children*

80 Maria Taylor Byrd (1698–1771)

Letter, September 6, 1745, to Mrs. Keir
Manuscript
3 pp. 9 x 7¼ in.

Maria Taylor, daughter of Thomas and Sarah Taylor of Kensington, England, became the second wife of William Byrd II (1674–1744) in 1724. Within several years she had moved to Virginia with him and remained there the rest of her life.

In this elegantly written, compassionate, and articulate letter, the recently widowed Maria Byrd commiserates with a correspondent identified only as Mrs. Keir, who had recently lost her own husband. She likewise reveals in some detail the trials of a woman suddenly burdened with the management of both her young family and her husband's vast estates. Her greatest concern, however, focuses on her only son, William Byrd III (1728–1777), "who was the Peculiar Care of his Father, and who lost Him at an Age, when most he stood in need of his prudent Councell to Steer him in a right Course." Maria Byrd confessed, "at some time I resolved to send him to your Island to compleat his Education, . . . and then I thought again he woud certainly get the Small-Pox, which is most terrible fatal to those who are born in America, and that I shoud be accessory to his Death." Ultimately, she placed her son at the College of William and Mary, where he would stay "till he became of Age."

Although she professed to have "no Attachments in this World of Sorrow for me to be Desirous of Longevity," Maria Byrd continued to live with her son and his family at Westover, from which this letter was written, until she died at the age of seventy-three.

ELS

I shoud be accessory to his Death, and then entreated Him at last to Stay till he became of age, of which he want Four year; and in the mean while I follow'd the Governours advice, to put him to our College under the Professor of Philosophy, a man of great Learning it seems. And now Madam pray give me your Advice as to Inoculation, woud you have me recommend that to Him? Do you think it right? or do you imagin it Presumption? I own this is takeing abundance of Liberty, and for which I ought to ask Pardon.

We in this part of the World are great Sufferers by the War, I have Sustaind very Considerable Losses since the Death of Mr Byrd by the Enemy; and am at this time under some Apprehention for our Fleet, haveing many Goods on Board, and none Insured, it was lately reported (But since contradicted) that our whole Fleet & Convoy was taken by the Brest Squadron, God knows whether this Rumour be true or false, 'tis time alone that must convince us.

Surely 'tis Marvellous to hear of a Persons takeing a new Lease of their Life at Eighty odd, it realy seems as if they woud continue upon Earth till the Millennium, or at least till they reach the Age of old Par, which Hystory tells us, was an Hundred and Threescore. There are no Attachments in this World

World of Sorrow for me to be Desirous of Longevity, and I compassionate those that bear the Burden of such a vast number of years upon their Shoulders.

I beg my kind Remembrance to Indamora and if my Eye-sight was not so much impaird as to make writing a Task to me, I shoud begin a Correspondence with Her.

I shoud rejoice to hear you had gaind the advantage of your Adversary, and am with much Respect & Devotion

Madam

Your most Obedient Humble Servant

Maria Byrd.

Westover the 6th of Sept 1745.

81 Augustus Köllner (1813–1906)

City Sights for Country Eyes
Philadelphia: American Sunday-School Union, 1856
12 plates

82 Augustus Köllner (1813–1906)

Common Sights in Town and Country
Philadelphia: American Sunday-School Union, 1850
12 plates

Augustus Köllner studied painting and lithography in Germany before he emigrated to America in 1839 and settled in Philadelphia. During the 1840s he traveled widely in the United States, making watercolor views of American scenes that were later lithographed and published as *Views of American Cities.*

Köllner also did work for the American Sunday-School Union. The ASSU vowed to establish a Sunday school in "every destitute place" and claimed that it published a book every Saturday. Most of these books were small, inexpensive, and crudely illustrated, until Köllner drew the plates for several of the children's books, most notably *City Sights for Country Eyes* and *Common Sights in Town and Country.* These genre drawings of everyday life were among his most accomplished and charming. *Common Sights* had twelve finely executed lithographs of Philadelphia scenes such as the village store, an oysterman selling his wares on the street, and a farmer at market. Each plate was accompanied by a page of text in large print that described the scene and pointed up a moral value.

FSP

From life, Phila.   Published by the American Sunday School Union,   Chestnut Street, Philadelphia.   A.Kollner. Lith? Phila.

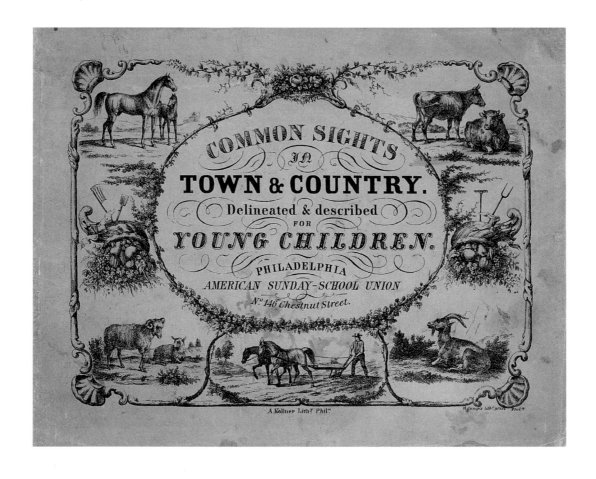

COMMON SIGHTS
IN
TOWN & COUNTRY.
Delineated & described
FOR
YOUNG CHILDREN.
PHILADELPHIA
AMERICAN SUNDAY-SCHOOL UNION
No 146 Chestnut Street.

A.Kollner Lith? Phil?   W.Camp's lith? press Phil?

83 Heinrich Hoffmann (1809–1894)

Slovenly Peter Reformed: Showing how he became a Neat Scholar
Philadelphia: W. P. Hazard, 1853
6 colorplates

> I tell of naughty girls and boys,
> Of ill-bred children, full of noise,
> Who play with lights and fire when able,—
> Who rock their chairs beside the table,
> 'Till falling down the dinner comes,—
> Who suck at once at both their thumbs
> Who would not let their nails be cut,
> Until at last so long they got,
> That from the hands away they stretched,
> Until the floor below they reached.

Heinrich Hoffmann, a German physician and writer, wrote his first book as a Christmas gift for his four-year-old son. He wrote five books in all, but he is best known for his creation of Slovenly Peter (Struwwelpeter). Hoffmann's cautionary tales featured a young boy whose wild appearance matched his unruly behavior. Parents may have found the illustrations disturbing, such as the one shown here of a mother using a saw to cut Peter's fingernails. But children found these hand-colored drawings humorous and just gruesome enough to be appealing.

FSP

84   J. H. Brown

Spectropia, or Surprising Spectral Illusions: Showing Ghosts Everywhere, and of any Colour
New York: James G. Gregory, 1864
11 pp. 16 plates

This book of illusionary images must have delighted its young audience when it was first published in 1863, although the compiler had a more serious purpose in mind. Alarmed by the growing interest in spiritualism, Brown maintained that this "mental epidemic" was caused by fraudulent mediums preying on a gullible public. He stated that his goal was "the extinction of the superstitious belief that apparitions are actual spirits, by showing some of the ways our senses may be deceived." He pointed out that all of the senses are more or less subject to deception, but "the eye is pre-eminently so." To prove his point, he instructed readers to focus their attention on the various ghostly plates in the book and then look at a blank wall. The image (or "specter") will reappear and vanish several times, and the colors of the plate will be reversed. He then concluded with a detailed explanation of the phenomenon of complementary afterimages and the persistence of vision.

For those people who prefer magic tricks to be performed without explanation, these simple illusions are perhaps more amusing in the absence of any further information.

FSP

SPECTROPIA

OR

SURPRISING

Spectral Illusions

SHOWING

GHOSTS

EVERYWHERE

AND OF ANY COLOUR.

NEW YORK:

PUBLISHED BY JAMES G. GREGORY,

540 Broadway.

85 Richard Henry Stoddard (1825–1903)

The Children in the Wood, Told in Verse
Illustrated by H. L. Stephens
New York: Hurd & Houghton, 1866
8 pp.

Also known as *The Babes in the Wood*, this children's story appeared as early as 1595 and was a favorite with minstrels. It was the tale of two orphaned children whose treacherous uncle abandoned them in the woods, where they starved to death. The uncle then inherited their estate, but he was ultimately punished for his wicked deed and thrown into prison. As he lay dying in the jail, he was tormented by the presence of two ghostly figures, "the phantoms of two children fair—The Children in the Wood!" This sentimental retelling of the story is by Richard Henry Stoddard, an American poet and literary critic. By all accounts, he had a miserable childhood, and perhaps he identified with the sad plight of the orphans in *The Children of the Wood.*

FSP

THE

Children in the Wood

TOLD IN VERSE

BY

RICHARD HENRY STODDARD

ILLUSTRATED

BY

H. L. STEPHENS

NEW YORK:
HURD & HOUGHTON,
401 BROADWAY,
1866.

86 S. L. Hill (manufacturer)

Marriage of Pocahontas & Rolfe

Williamsburgh, New York: ca. 1868

 Puzzle of twenty wooden blocks with colored paper surfaces. 7¾ x 5⁴⁄₅ x ⅞ in.

Renowned in her lifetime for traveling to England as a Christianized Indian, Pocahontas (1595–1617) was again celebrated two centuries later when Americans remembered their nation's colonial history. At that time she was venerated both for her baptism into the Anglican church and for saving the life of the English captain John Smith, who had emerged as an American hero shortly after the birth of the new republic. The British expatriate writer John Davis, active at the turn into the nineteenth century, was the first to embellish the story of the rescue by adding a tale of romantic love between Pocahontas and Smith. That appealing mythology would be perpetuated for the next two hundred years.

Pocahontas actually married John Rolfe, not John Smith, a fact that was made known to many in 1855 by a popular engraving, Henry Brueckner's "Marriage of Pocahontas," published in New York, London, and Edinburgh. The wedding is in fact poorly documented. Brueckner invented details that no doubt were the inspiration for this block puzzle, produced on Long Island; the puzzle takes from the engraving elements of the setting, composition, and treatment of several figures. An inscription in pencil on the box of the puzzle provides the date 1868.

The Pocahontas story has long been cherished by children. Contemporary with the puzzle, and perhaps also influenced by Brueckner's print, is *The Royal Illuminated Book of Legends* (Edinburgh, 1872), which presents "Pocahontas: A Tale of Old Virginie" in company with stories about King Alfred, Puss in Boots, and The Hind of the Forest.

WMSR

MARRIAGE OF POCAHONTAS & ROLFE.

S.L. Hill, Manufacturer, Nos 80 & 82 South Seventh Street Williamsburgh

87   Author unknown

The Home Primer
New York: McLouglin Bro's., ca. 1887
32 pp.

Children have learned their ABCs from primers for hundreds of years. The colonists brought these precious little books with them to this country, and by 1690 *The New England Primer* was being published, the first of many American primers. These early ones taught moral edification and religious lessons, and primers were considered almost as important as the Bible in molding the character of children. The primers contained a rhyming alphabet, prayers to be memorized, and basic reading material selected to turn "young vipers" into responsible citizens.

Later the name "primer" was given to all elementary books for children. By the time this primer was published, dour lessons had given way to stories emphasizing the Victorian family and the social role of children. In Lesson 28 of *The Home Primer*, young readers are told that "a child often looks forward to manhood, and dreams of the pleasures of older people, with feelings that they are greater than any that it enjoys. But this is a mistake. Childhood is the play day of life."

FSP

THE HOME PRIMER.

88   L. Frank Baum (1856–1919)

The Army Alphabet

Illustrations by Harry Kennedy

Chicago, New York: George M. Hill Company, 1900

30 leaves

Alphabet books have amused and instructed children for centuries. They represent one of the earliest uses of pictures in instructional books for students, starting in the sixteenth century with the hornbooks or wooden paddles with inscribed alphabets, numerals, and prayers. Out of this tradition came the battledore, a folded piece of cardboard with an illustrated alphabet.

By the time L. Frank Baum published this alphabet book, printing technology had developed to the point at which children expected their books to be in bold and irresistible color.

Baum's career as a children's author began when his family encouraged him to compile the nursery rhymes he told his sons. His first book, *Mother Goose in Prose*, sold well, and he followed with *Father Goose: His Book*, which became the best-selling children's title of 1899. In 1900 he had two books published. *The Army Alphabet*, an over-sized picture book, taught the alphabet with illustrations from the Spanish-American War era. The second book, *The Wonderful Wizard of Oz*, quickly achieved the status of an American classic.

FSP

F represents the starry FLAG
For which our soldiers fight.
When on the battle-field it waves
It is a glorious sight,
And every one who sees it knows
Our cause is surely right.

HK.

IX. *Old Dominion, New Nation*

89 Edward Randolph (ca. 1632–1703)

"A Journall Since the Tyme of My Arrivall in Virginia from ye 5 of Aprill 1692 to the 12 July 1695"
Manuscript
5 pp. 7¾ x 11½ in.

Edward Randolph appears to have been the consummate British bureaucrat. Educated at Gray's Inn, London, he spent most of his life in government service. Favored by both Charles II and James II, Randolph somehow managed to land on his feet following England's Glorious Revolution. King William and Queen Mary dispatched him in 1692 with the ponderous title of "Surveyor General of Their Majesties' Customs in All the Provinces and Colonies on the Continent of America." He was likewise burdened with the thankless tasks of attempting to enforce the Navigation Acts and to curb the smuggling that ran rampant along the North American coastline.

Randolph's daily entries, crafted in his minute script, are brief but packed with fascinating detail about his extensive time in Virginia, his travels along the east coast, and his observations of American commerce in general, especially in the Chesapeake Bay region. Randolph encountered numerous obstacles to fulfilling his mission, mostly in the form of colonial officials, from Tidewater sheriffs all the way to the governor of Maryland. His travels also placed him in a position to observe history in the making, as when he visited Salem, Massachusetts, on September 22, 1692, and witnessed firsthand the last hanging of alleged witches in that village.

Papers generated by Randolph as a colonial administrator were collected and published at the turn of the twentieth century. This journal, which was then—and until much later—unknown to scholars, complements those published materials nicely. Diaries kept in America in the seventeenth century remain extremely rare.

ELS

A Journall since the hour of my arrivall in Virginia from ye 5 of Aprill, 1692 to the 12 July, 1692 —

(5) Landed at James T. (15) informed Gov: Copley of a ship from Ireland & 2 from Scotl.d desiring him to seize them (16) prosecuted merchy vessell. Reved (22) Co.tt Scarburgh made Co.tt of Accomack. (23) left James T. went towards S.t Maryes. May (1) came to S.t Maryes (100 M) (7) hired boat to go to C. Blackistons, prevented by bad wind. (8) hired horses, went to his house, pretended he was bound to S.t Maryes, did nothing more, went to Patuxent (45 M) (10) went aboard Jo. Laird loding tobacco in that river. (11) went to S.t Maryes (12) hearing C. Hinch was upp ye Bay I wrote letters to him to prevent carrying tobacco over land out of Maryl.d to delaware. (13) demanded of Mr Blacks W.t Blacks bond he would not lett me see it (14) I wrote that neither he Jones or Quin might be cleared till he was satisfied in ye security (15) Mr Black cleared vessells would not bill me their names (16) I had notice Massey from London & Crooks hawks from Ireland but both from S.t were loding tobacco on ye E: shore (20) I wrote by Bay (23) seized Massey (27) seized Crooks hawks (31) I returned to S.t Maryes. June (1) a spirituall C. came to buy them (2) cast in Masseys cause ye C. would not have another guess bye Crooks hawks...

...July (9) an Aud.t now (10) with Coll: Nich. to Wiquetan (11) aboard Snow. (10) with Comadore C. Marshall killed by 2 of his men. ye Comadore C. Marshall killed by 2 of his men. (12:13:14) visited ye ships in the fleet at S.t Comfort. found Glanvill & Goffe now wrote to ye Comm: to send his boat & hands to unbend their sayles and carry them to ye Co.tt ashore. they stole away that night (17) had Jo. Laird of Donnacade crossed to give better security. (19) the fleet 109 sayle went giue better security. (24) gaue C. Hinch order in writing to bring to S.ta (24) gaue C. Hinch order in writing to bring Massey & Crooks hawks at 1. that afternoon went by water to Palux (22) mett Mr Black at S.t Maryes by water to Palux. (23) promised to stay till my returne went to Palux.

(4) to Widdow Tours house (5) to N. Castle (100 M) (5) to Philp: (9) to Burlington (10) hired horse for N. york (12) came thither fell sick short. (24) at N. yorke. (30) Landed sick at R. Island. (1) Sloop hired (2) came to Boston (3) ill by S.W. (7) delivered him a copy of some Articles of my instruction. (13) to Piscataq. examined ye Officers books. a vessell seized by Mr Beoulton ye salt was seized (21) returned by Salem saw ye Officers books found Mr Black certific: for tobacco. (22) & gave say hanged there. (23) to Boston examined Mr Brintons books had certific: of Black for tobacco. he went to R. Island. Oct: (1) not returned could have no acc.t of his seizures (6) at 4 that afternoon I left Boston (7: 8: 9) thence to New London seized two Sloop Supply the Scotch goods were putt aboard by Hithen would not let me prosecute him (100 M) (10:11) to Hartford ordered ye Sloop to be prosecuted (60 M) (12) to Stonehouse, to Wallingford, N. haven. Milford, Stratford Fairfield Norwalk. Stamford East chester (15) to N york late at night (132 M) Coll Fletcher Gov.r was arrived. (22) left N. york. to Eliz: town. (25) to Philp. 102 M: (26) to Upland Brandewine creek Christian creek to N. Castle (40 M) (28) to Adam Petersons to duck creek to Motherkill No: (1) to ye Horekill. 100 M: (3) to M.rs Scotts to James Roands to G. Layfields at Pocomoke (41 M) by Guffs at ferryes. (7) I heard a vessell from Surry was arrived at harding creek. (9:10:11:12:13) crossed ye Bay this Mr (14) to Coll Darnell. Coll: pyd to Nanze Bay this Mr (14) to Coll Darnell. crossed ye river to upper machodick work on Potom: crossed ye river to upper machodick to Coll Jennings to James To: having passed Patux. Potom: ye river 209 M. Feb (3) left James To: to Coll: Colts Potom: ye river to M.rs Wilsons passed James R. (6:7:8) violent storm to M.rs Wilsons passed James R. (11) passed James R. to Mich.ll & returned to Mr Wilsons. (11) passed James R. to Mich.ll to Cap: Thruston to Mr Lowrie & to R: baughams at Gilbert point (50 M) (14) to Evan Jones in N. Caroli. to Mr Jarvis Lt: Gov: (16) in a canoe to Paulico. to paniskeig another Indian town of 11 cabins. thence over passibtanck to Mr Musi. at Little river thence a dismall Swamp. examined his scattered papers being newly come to that place (18) to ye Widdow Clocks (19:20:21) to Evan Jones (23) to Eliz: To: (24) to Coll Lears directed him ye method to keep his books paue: etc. (26) to C: Powells to Mr Edwards to James To: Jan.y (3) to Coll: Lightfoots ye Comp: found his books in great disorder assisted him Comp: found his books in great disorder assisted him (5) to Coll: Hill directed him ye methods of his books (7) to Coll: Birds ye Aud: to enquire after their Ma.ty (9) to Coll Birds ye Aud: seized & condemned by C. Custis third parts of 3 vessells seized & condemned by C. Custis (4) dispersed a Mem.ll to S.t E. R. & Councill to have a vessell fitted for me to look after illegall traders (4) a vessell fitted for me to look after illegall trade Cap. Hinch frigatt disabled for want of Anchors Cap. Hinch was ordred to find out a fitting...

90   Richard Traunter

"The Travels of Richard Traunter on the Main Continent of America from Appomattox River in Virginia to Charles Town in South Carolina"
Manuscript volume
74 pp. 8½ x 13 in.

Richard Traunter's journals of his two expeditions to find a shorter overland trade route from Virginia to the South Carolina coast in 1698 and 1699 provide a detailed, if self-serving, account of the author's adventures. Written in a remarkably legible early-eighteenth-century hand and dedicated to Charles, Lord Halifax, of the British Privy Council, the journals recount a remarkable trek totaling more than fifteen hundred miles. Touting the support of Col. William Byrd I for his journeys, Traunter recorded descriptions of the land over which he traveled, the flora and fauna he encountered, and the Native American people with whom he interacted, including revealing accounts of their living conditions, society, and customs. He particularly emphasized his own role in "making peace with several Nations of Indians, to the great advantage of the Indian Traders in those parts, by opening a way that had not been travell'd before." Although white accounts of Indian contact must always be approached with some caution—and Traunter's are particularly self-congratulatory—his do provide valuable perspectives on Native Americans in this region and time.

The journals are bound with several other contemporary documents, including a memorial of Traunter and Edward Loughton to the Lords Commissioners for Trade and Plantations concerning the encouragement of future exploration, along with accounts of the discovery of gold and silver mines in the Carolinas, each of which also sounds a persistent set of complaints against the colonial officials of South Carolina for interfering with the efforts of the traders-explorers.

ELS

THE

TRAVELS

of

RICHARD TRAUNTER

on the Main Continent of America
from Appomattox River in Virginia
to Charles Town in South
Carolina ·

In two Journals; performed
in the Years 1698: and 1699: ✳

Wherin is Contained the Quality & Nature
of the Soyle, the Disposition of the Inhabitants
and the Reception I had amongst them; Also my
making Peace with several Nations of Indians
to the great advantage of the Indian Traders
in those parts, by opening a way that had not been
Travell'd before; with what else Remarkably Occur'd
in my way · ✳

91   Hugh Jones (1699–1760)

The Present State of Virginia Giving A particular and short Account of the Indians, English and Negroe Inhabitants of that Colony . . .
London: Printed for J. Clarke, at the *Bible*, under the *Royal-Exchange*, 1724
viii, 151 pp.

After the absurd propagandist literature of the first decades, Virginia came under much criticism in the ensuing years. To combat "very erroneous and monstrous Thoughts" (p. vi) held in England about the colony, a young Anglican clergyman wrote *The Present State of Virginia* in 1724.

Hugh Jones had left Jesus College at Oxford in 1717 to become professor of mathematics at the College of William and Mary in Virginia. Later he would become chaplain to the House of Burgesses. He reported how, by 1724, Virginia had "far more advanced and improved in all Respects . . . than in the whole Century before" (p. ii). His generally positive account concluded that Virginia was "the most antient and loyal" and "the most extensive and beneficial Colony belonging to the Crown of Great Britain" (p. 47).

Jones pointed out that "Arts, Sciences, Trades, and useful Inventions are now planted" in Virginia (p. iii). He observed with favor that the gentry were pursuing the finer things of life and that "The Habits, Life, Customs, Computations &c. of the Virginians are much the same as about London, which they esteem their Home" (p. 43). Yet, he saw deficiencies and supplemented his descriptive chapters with three appendices that were comprehensive programs for improving education, religious observance, and trade.

Without knowing it, Jones was reporting the beginning of the golden age of Virginia's tobacco plantation economy, a period of relative stability that followed the formative years of the colony's development. As we know now, however, that society began to be undermined just as it reached maturity a few decades later. Jones assured his readers that "There can be no Room for real Apprehension of Danger of a Revolt of the Plantation in future Ages" (p. 146). Yet, within half a century of the appearance of his volume, the process of maturation that he reported resulted in Virginia's declaring its independence.

JCK

THE
PRESENT STATE
OF
VIRGINIA.

GIVING

A particular and short Account of the *Indian, English,* and *Negroe* Inhabitants of that Colony.

Shewing their Religion, Manners, Government, Trade, Way of Living, *&c.* with a Description of the Country.

From whence is inferred a short VIEW of

MARYLAND *and* NORTH CAROLINA.

To which are added,

Schemes and Propositions for the better Promotion of Learning, Religion, Inventions, Manufactures, and Trade in *Virginia,* and the other *Plantations.*

For the Information of the *Curious,* and for the Service of such as are engaged in the *Propagation of the Gospel* and *Advancement of Learning,* and for the Use of all Persons concerned in the

Virginia Trade and Plantation.

GEN. ix. 27.

God shall enlarge JAPHETH, *and he shall dwell in the Tents of* SHEM, *and* CANAAN *shall be his Servant.*

By *HUGH JONES,* A. M. Chaplain to the Honourable Assembly, and lately Minister of *James-Town,* &c. in *Virginia.*

LONDON:

Printed for J. CLARKE, at the *Bible* under the *Royal-Exchange.* MDCCXXIV.

92 Walter Hoxton

To the Merchants of London Trading to Virginia and Maryland, This Mapp of the Bay of Chesepeack, with the Rivers Potowmack, Potaspsco, North East and part of Chester, is Humbly Dedicated and Presented
London: W. Betts and E. Baldwin, ca. 1750
4 sheets. 36½ x 55 in. (assembled)

Walter Hoxton captained a tobacco ship in the 1720s and 1730s for the London mercantile firm of John and Samuel Hyde. During the course of some two dozen voyages to the Chesapeake Bay, he charted numerous channels and shoals and identified navigational landmarks. Combining his own observations with information from older, less reliable maps, Hoxton produced in 1735 his detailed *Mapp of the Bay of Chesepeack*, a work clearly created by a mariner for other seafarers who traversed the waters off the coast of the Maryland and Virginia colonies.

Hoxton's map offered its users a great variety of useful information, but the prescient mariner also recognized the realities of a constantly changing coastline resulting from the continual ebb and flow of coastal waters. Thus, he left space for other seamen to enter their own observations for future use. Anticipating the work of Benjamin Franklin and others, he also included his own *"Attempt* towards Ascertaining the Limits Course & Strength of the *North East Current* on the Coast of Virginia," so that mariners might take advantage of the Gulf Stream on voyages northward or avoid it as they traveled southward along the coast.

The value of Hoxton's map may be discerned from the fact that so few of his original edition survive, suggesting that copies were worn out in use (although relatively few may have actually been produced). A second, and equally rare, edition was issued around 1750 (the version shown here), and the contents of the map were frequently plagiarized over the ensuing quarter-century.

ELS

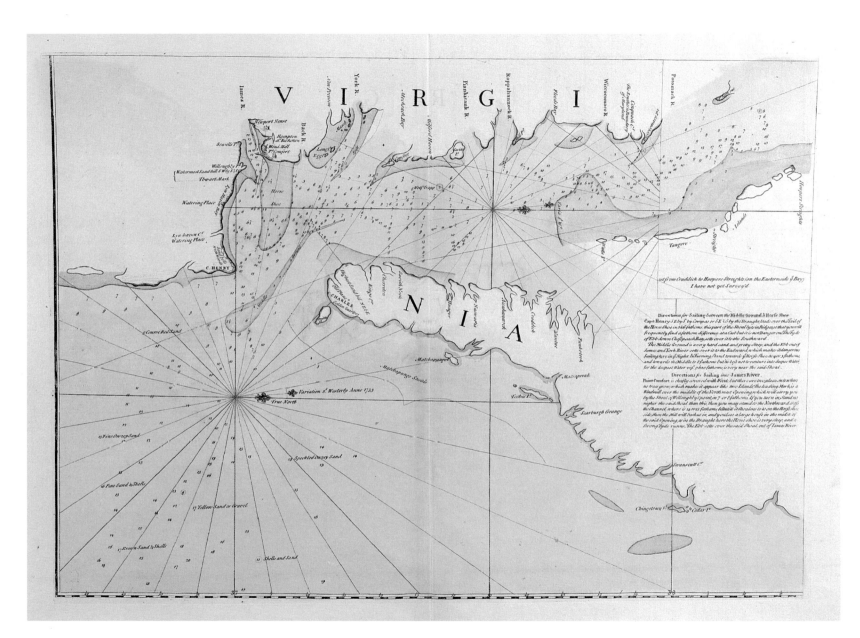

93　Thomas Jefferson (1743–1826)

Observations Sur La Virginie, Par M. J***. Traduites de L'Anglois
Paris: Chez Barrois, L'Aîne, Librarie, Rue Hurepoix, Près Le Pont Saint-Michel, 1786
390 pp.

Notes on Virginia provides indispensable commentary on various aspects of American life and history during the last decades of the eighteenth century. In addition to factual notations on the flora, fauna, and natural history of Virginia, Thomas Jefferson discusses religious freedom, the separation of church and state, theories on art and education, his attitudes toward slavery, and his interest in science.

Desiring to amass reliable information on the American states, François Marbois, the secretary of the French legation at Philadelphia, circulated a semi-official questionnaire among members of the Continental Congress in 1780. One set of queries made its way into Thomas Jefferson's able hands.

Jefferson returned his replies to Marbois by late 1780. The manuscript was privately published in an edition of two hundred in May 1785. The edition was published without Jefferson's name on the title page and was given by the publisher the title by which it became known, *Notes on Virginia*. Intended solely for private distribution, one of the copies, however, fell into the hands of the French bookseller Barrois. Faced with the prospect of unauthorized publication, Jefferson cooperated, hoping to mitigate the damage. The resulting edition, actually published early in 1787, however, was far from successful. Numerous misprints and errors of translation mar the edition. The order of the material is changed. Even the date on the title page is incorrect, claiming that the original was printed in 1782 rather than 1785.

Jefferson's response was to strike a hurried deal with English bookseller and publisher John Stockdale, sending him a carefully corrected manuscript. Stockdale was swift and efficient. That edition was published in the summer of 1787. All subsequent editions published during Jefferson's lifetime were based on Stockdale's book. Although Jefferson once referred to it as "nothing more than the measure of a shadow," *Notes on Virginia* provides insight into author as well as subject and is a minor classic of American literature.

BCG

OBSERVATIONS

SUR *9575*

LA VIRGINIE,

PAR M. J***.

TRADUITES DE L'ANGLOIS.

Th. Jefferson

9/158

A PARIS,

Chez BARROIS, l'aîné, Libraire, rue du
Hurepoix, près le pont Saint-Michel.

———

1786.

94 Joseph Clinton Robertson (1788–1852) and Thomas Byerley (d. 1826) (pseud. Sholto Percy and Reuben Percy), compilers

The Percy Anecdotes
London: Printed for T. Boys, 1820–23
20 vols. (incomplete set: vols. 10–20 wanting)

95 John Forster (1812–1876)

The Life and Times of Oliver Goldsmith
London: Bradbury and Evans, 1855
xl, 472 pp.

Fore-edge paintings are miniature paintings that decorate the unbound edge of a book. The picture cannot be seen when the volume is closed but can be seen by fanning the leaves open. Fanning shifts the position of the leaves, causing each page to expose a minute margin of the page beneath it. The artist paints on the fore-edge while the text block is clamped in the fanned-out position. After the paint has dried, the binder applies gilt over the fore-edge. Fore-edge painting is called the "curious" art or the "lost" art because the picture painted on the edges is lost when the book is in a normal closed position.

This form of book decoration became popular in America in the nineteenth century, when tourists to Britain purchased these books and brought them back to this country. The paintings often depicted English castles and landscapes, and gradually American picturesque scenes began to appear. In many cases, the illustrations were unrelated to the content of the book, as with the books displayed here. The ten volumes of the *Percy Anecdotes* (a miscellaneous collection of articles that originally came out in forty-four monthly parts) all have fore-edge paintings of Virginia scenes, chiefly of the Richmond area ("the old Stone House, Richmond, Va."; "view on James River above Richmond, Va."; "James River from Mayo's Bridge"; "Rocks and hills near Moorfield, Va."; "Karr's Pinnacles and Cathedral Rock, Va. U.S.A."; "The Crawford Monument and a view of the tomb of Monroe, Richmond, Va." (opposite, top); "The Peaks of Otter, Va."; "View on the New River, Va."; "Ruins of Richmond, Virginia after the War"). *The Life and Times of Oliver Goldsmith* was presented in 1856 as a prize to a student at Chatham House Academy, Ramsgate. Presumably, the fore-edge painting of "Fortress Monroe, Va. U.S.A." (opposite, bottom) was painted later.

FSP

96 William Russell Birch (1755–1834)

The Country Seats of the United States of North America, with some Scenes connected with them
Springland near Bristol, Pennsylvania: Designed and Published by W. Birch, Enamel
Painter, 1808[-09]
20 colorplates

William Birch exhibited miniature and watercolor paintings in London for twenty years before he emigrated to Philadelphia in 1794. In 1791 he engraved *Delices de la Grande Bretagne*, a copperplate book of the type that he would introduce to America with *The City of Philadelphia* (1800), a volume that celebrated what Birch called the "eminence" of the new American capital.

Country Seats of the United States is an early pictorial record of rural buildings and of a storied river, the Schuylkill. Thirteen of its twenty plates are given to architecture or scenery near Philadelphia. Birch stated that the purpose of the publication was to promote "Taste" in architecture and landscape design, and thereby favorably shape the character of the new nation and establish its "respectability." In actuality, the artist was driven as much by a personal motive. Having immigrated for the opportunity to join the gentry, he had purchased near Philadelphia his own estate, Springland, the grounds of which he pictured in two plates in *Country Seats* as evidence of his own taste and social status. The house at Springland drained Birch financially and was never completed. At least partly for that reason the artist stressed "the beauty of the situation" of any country seat over "the massy magnitude of the edifice."

Pictured here is "Mount Vernon, Virginia, the Seat of the late Genl. G. Washington" (copperplate engraving with hand coloring, 4 x 5⅜ in.). Typically, Birch's view shows off the landscape, with the Potomac River prominent in the distance. "This hallowed mansion is founded upon a rocky eminence, a dignified height on the Potomac," Birch writes in introducing the view. As seen here, the artist worked his copperplates with line and stipple engraving, then hand colored the prints to create appealing detail and color.

WMSR

Mount Vernon, *Virginia, the Seat of the late* Gen.¹ G. Washington.

Drawn Engraved & Published by W. Birch Springland near Bristol Pennsylv.ᵃ

97A William Guy Wall (1792–after 1864)

The Hudson River Portfolio
New York: Henry G. Megarey, 1821–25
2 vols. 20 colorplates

The *Hudson River Portfolio* is considered the finest colorplate book produced in nineteenth-century America. This series of twenty large views of scenery, each magnificently rendered, records the natural beauty of the landscape and the patterns of settlement along the Hudson River in the early 1820s. The portfolio was the work of two immigrants whose foreign training underlies the quality of the project and its success. The views were drawn by William Guy Wall, a native of Dublin and a watercolorist. Wall settled in America in 1818 to become a founder in New York City of the National Academy of Design, where he would exhibit. The views were engraved by John Hill, an established artist in London who emigrated to Philadelphia in 1816. In the years 1820–21 Hill prepared the plates for Joshua Shaw's landmark *Picturesque Views of American Scenery*; the *Hudson River Portfolio* soon followed. The plates of both volumes were hand-colored aquatint engravings. Few artists in America ever attempted the medium because of its difficulty and expense.

The upper reaches of the Hudson River were characterized by wilderness scenery commingled with the buildings and bridges of early settlement. Wall selected a series of views of falls, which appealed to him for the sublimity of their fury. Pictured here is his depiction of "Baker's Falls" (13⅞ x 20⅝ in.), which shows the pristine grandeur of unspoiled nature, notably in the water, rugged rocks, and rigid trees. A handsome mill is evidence that man has sufficiently tamed this landscape to live comfortably there. Hill's colors are clean and crisp; his details are sharp.

WMSR

BAKER'S FALLS.

(No. 8) of the Hudson River Port Folio.

Published by Henry I. Megarey New York.

97B   William Guy Wall (1792–after 1864)

The Hudson River Portfolio
New York: Henry G. Megarey, 1821–25
2 vols. 20 colorplates

William Guy Wall's ambitious portfolio of twenty landscape views that celebrate a specific region adapted a European tradition to a New World setting. The portfolio follows the progress of the Hudson River as it flows southward 315 miles from the Adirondack Mountains to the harbor of New York City. The first plates present the scenery of the headwaters, which in the 1820s remained partly wilderness; its many falls and rapids seemed sublime to the eyes of Europeans. For the lower half of the river's course, the scenery became more picturesque, with evidence of man's idyllic settlement in such towns as Hudson, Newburg, and Troy. The valley of the Hudson was soon to inspire the development of a school of painters who envisioned this landscape as God's gift to a favored people. Wall's *Hudson River Portfolio* anticipated that significant movement in American art. Although he approached the land with an Old World interest in the extremes of dramatic and pastoral scenery, Wall's imagery as engraved by John Hill often captures the purity and clarity of the American landscape and atmosphere, just as would the later Hudson River School painters.

Pictured here is the town of Hudson, near Catskill, which lies midway along the river (aquatint with hand coloring, 14 x 21⅛ in.). Hudson in the 1820s seemed an Arcadia, a prosperous community of handsome mills, churches, and houses gracefully set in a vast yet tranquil landscape that is bathed in sunlight. Wall and Hill interpret the settlement as man and nature in perfect harmony. Broad horizontals of landscape, the gentle flow of the river, the simple geometry of the town's architecture, and Hill's exquisite rendering of detail and light all serve to convey serenity.

WMSR

Painted by W.G. Wall.

Engraved by I. Hill.

HUDSON.

N.º 13) of the Hudson River Port Folio

Published by Henry I. Megarey New York.

98 A. A. Turner

Villas on the Hudson. A Collection of Photo-Lithographs of Thirty one Country Residences
New York: D. Appleton, 1860
55 pp. 31 colorplates

    Villas on the Hudson was the first large-scale and successful publication in the United States to feature photo-lithography. The new technique wedded photography and lithography to produce a colored photolithograph, to which additional tinting (here, brown and green) was applied by means of stencil blocks. The result was a sensational visual effect. In terms of the quality of imagery, *Villas on the Hudson* compared favorably with contemporary English publications, surpassing, for example, Pouncy's *Dorsetshire Photographically Illustrated* (London and Dorchester, 1857), the plates of which were heavily retouched by hand.

    A. A. Turner set out to update William Guy Wall's *Hudson River Portfolio* (q.v.), the finest American colorplate book, which features the natural landscape of the famous river, by depicting instead thirty of the mansions newly erected along its banks. This river is a "pleasant land to see," Turner states in his preface, but even more remarkable, he implies, is "the state of rural, architectural embellishment on the Hudson." In actuality, the giant Gothic castles and Italian villas built at midcentury by "a wealthy and cultivated portion of our citizens" are for the most part little distinguished in design, despite their authorship by such accomplished figures as Gervaise Wheeler, Detlef Lienau, and A. J. Davis. The buildings are simply large, designed that way to accommodate the tastes of nouveau riche patrons. Many of these palaces were photographed in 1858 and 1859, when they were newly completed and little landscaped. Pictured here is the "Residence of S. D. Babcock, Riverdale."

WMSR

Residence of **S. D. BABCOCK.**
Riverdale

99   John James Audubon (1785–1851) and Rev. John Bachman (1790–1874)

The Viviparous Quadrupeds of North America
New York: J. J. Audubon, 1845–48
3 vols. 150 colored plates

Following the success of his *Birds of America*, John James Audubon began to gather material for an equally ambitious project to document the animal life of North America. The results of the artist-naturalist's years of research and field study was the *Viviparous Quadrupeds of North America*, the outstanding work on American mammals of its time and a superb example of color lithography. Audubon included many frontier animals never before depicted, and his landmark publication helped foster a public appreciation of American nature.

Audubon collaborated with the Reverend John Bachman, a Lutheran minister and experienced student of mammalogy, who later wrote much of the scientific text. Audubon collected specimens sent to him by friends, and in 1843 he made a final expedition up the Missouri River to do more fieldwork. He envisioned *Viviparous Quadrupeds* (literally meaning four-footed mammals bearing live offspring) as the definitive record of all North American mammals. Bachman warned Audubon, who was not a trained naturalist, that he had underestimated the scope of the mammal population, and they agreed to eliminate bats and marine animals. By 1846 Audubon's health was failing, and his son John Woodhouse made substantial artistic contributions, eventually completing half the plates for *Quadrupeds*. Another son, Victor, served as editor and business manager.

Despite the difficulty of marketing colorplate books in America, *Quadrupeds* was a commercial success and was published in two sizes and several editions between 1845 and 1854. The elephant folio edition shown here contains a number of animals from Virginia, such as these plates of the "Virginian Opossum Female and Young male, 7 months old natural size" and "Common or Virginian Deer. Old Male & Female."

FSP

PLATE LXVI.

DIDELPHIS VIRGINIANA, PENNANT.
VIRGINIAN OPOSSUM.

PLATE CXXXVI.

CERVUS VIRGINIANUS, PENNANT.
COMMON OR VIRGINIAN DEER.

100 Edwin Sheppard (1837–1904) [and William Ludwell Sheppard (1833–1912)]

"The Birds of Virginia, U. S., Drawn from Nature," compiled 1850–55
Manuscript volume
56 pp.

Edwin Sheppard was the younger brother of the Richmond artist William Ludwell Sheppard. After schooling at Bowling Green, Edwin by age seventeen was a topographical engineer with the York River Railway. He served as an officer of engineers in the Confederate army. After the Civil War he was employed as a scientific draftsman by the Smithsonian Institution and for twenty-five years as a draftsman of natural history specimens by the Academy of Natural Sciences in Philadelphia. He illustrated *The History of North American Birds* in 1874, *North American Shore Birds* in 1895, and drew fifty-eight portraits of fowl for *American Duck Shooting* in 1901. Although the present volume of fifty-six watercolors appears to be a book, having both an index and title page—reading "By Edwin Sheppard/Philadelphia, 1850–5"—it never was published. The dates "1850–5" are those of execution, and these watercolors are Sheppard's earliest known works.

Although only Edwin's name appears on the title page, eleven watercolors with elaborate landscape backgrounds are minutely signed "WLS Del." (William Ludwell Sheppard Delineator). There is no doubt, however, that Edwin painted the birds themselves. William's diary (at the Library of Virginia) for October 14, 1853, reads, "Went to the Library and saw Audubon's Birds; I think that Eddie's are superior to some of them." On October 30 he wrote, "Eddie stayed at home to finish a bird he had commenced in the country."

In the late 1850s William's work was noticed by one of John James Audubon's artist sons, possibly John Woodhouse Audubon. As a result, William went to Europe in 1860, and his diary suggests that he went to recruit a lithographer for an unspecified project. Could it have been "The Birds of Virginia"? Such a project certainly would have appealed to a son of John James Audubon, being conceived as the Virginia equivalent of Audubon's *The Birds of America*.

JCK

101 Edward Beyer (1820–1865)

The Album of Virginia or Illustration of the Old Dominion
[Richmond,] Virginia: Ed. Beyer, 1858
Lithographs by Rau & son, Dresden, and W. Locillot, Berlin
40 colorplates

From 1848 to 1857, the German landscapist Edward Beyer was active in America, where he traveled as far west as Cincinnati. In Virginia, Beyer prepared sketches for an ambitious colorplate book with forty views. His stated purpose with the *Album of Virginia* was "to illustrate the natural curiosities, the favorite resorts of pleasure and health, and many of the triumphs of art and skill, as developed by the improvements in the State." Beyer devoted eighteen plates to Virginia's "natural curiosities," including multiple views of Natural Bridge and the Peaks of Otter. Nearly as many of the plates, fifteen, record the appearance of the world-famous mineral and thermal springs of the Old Dominion, those "favorite resorts of pleasure and health." Seven plates, plus the title page, picture such "triumphs of art and skill" as two bridges, a tunnel, a canal, a hotel, and two armories.

Pictured here is "Harper's Ferry from Jefferson Rock" (lithograph, 10¾ x 17¾ in.), which appears second in the *Album*, following a view of Natural Bridge. Notes published to accompany the *Album* (written probably by Samuel Mordecai) describe the scenery there as "perhaps, the most singularly picturesque in America" and explain that "the Rock [located to the right in the illustration] was a favorite resort of [Thomas] Jefferson, affording a magnificent view of the junction of the two Rivers, and of the thriving and beautiful village."

The plates of the *Album of Virginia* were printed in subdued colors. Some copies, however, including this exceptionally fine one owned by Paul Mellon, were greatly enhanced by hand coloring to produce rich imagery akin to Beyer's oil paintings.

WMSR

Taken from Nature by Ed. Beyer.   Entered according to Act of Congress in the year 1857 by Ed. Beyer in the Clerks Office of the District of Virginia.   Rau & Son. Lith. Dresden.

HARPER'S FERRY from JEFFERSON ROCK

JEFFERSON C.º V.ª

102 Lefevre James Cranstone (ca. 1820–1867)

"Rippon [Ripon] Hall, York River, Va.," 1860
Watercolor on paper. 11¾ x 6 in.

    Lefevre James Cranstone (active U.S. 1859–60) was a talented and prolific English painter. Probably born in London in 1820, Cranstone worked as a professional artist as early as 1845. Although it is not known where he trained, between 1845 and 1867 he exhibited paintings at London's most prestigious galleries, including the Society of British Artists, the Royal Academy, and the British Institution. Cranstone lived in various parts of England, eventually settling in Australia, where he died in 1867.

    This watercolor depicts a lonely, evocative scene. The partially planted fields barely reveal any growth. A dirt road, its margins encroached upon by weedy grass, sees far less traffic than when it was constructed and the adjacent fields fenced. In the distance is the seat of the plantation, Ripon Hall, and beyond it the York River. Ripon Hall was the estate of Edmund Jenings, instrumental in laying out the nearby town of Williamsburg; attorney general; a member, secretary, then president of the Council; and twice lieutenant governor of the colony. Neighboring plantations on the south side of the York included Porto Bello, the seat of Lord Dunmore, and Ringfield; immediately across the river were Timberneck, Rosewell, and Fairfield. By the time Cranstone recorded this scene, the first Ripon Hall had been replaced by the early- to mid-nineteenth-century brick structure illustrated here, also called Ripon Hall.

    Cranstone's melancholy scene contrasts the swaggering power of Virginia's Revolutionary-era Tidewater gentry with the exhausted fields and sputtering rural economy of the antebellum period.

BCG

CONTRIBUTORS

ACd   Ann C. de Witt, Research Assistant, Publications Department

BCG   Bryan Clark Green, Associate Curator for Prints and Photographs

JCK   James C. Kelly, Assistant Director for Museums

NDL   Nelson D. Lankford, Assistant Director for Publications and Education and Virginius Dabney Editor, *Virginia Magazine of History and Biography*

LLL   Lauranett L. Lee, Curator of African American History

PAL   Paul A. Levengood, Associate Editor, *Virginia Magazine of History and Biography*

FSP   Frances S. Pollard, Assistant Director for Library Services

WMSR   William M. S. Rasmussen, Lora M. Robins Curator of Art

ELS   E. Lee Shepard, Assistant Director for Manuscripts and Archives and Sallie and William B. Thalhimer III Senior Archivist

RFS   Robert F. Strohm, Associate Director and Paul Mellon Curator of Rare Books

Photography by Ron Jennings, except as follows:

Frontispiece, "Paul Mellon," photo courtesy National Gallery of Art, Washington, D.C.

"Paul Mellon in front of the Brick House" (p. x), photo by Heinz Kluetmeier, courtesy *Sports Illustrated.*

"The Old Library in the Brick House" (p. xi), by Steve Tucker, courtesy Estate of Paul Mellon.